W9-ACR-673

Betty Crocker's
MICROWAVE
COOKING

Director of Photography: Remo Cosentino

Golden Press/New York
Western Publishing Company, Inc.
Racine, Wisconsin

Revised Edition
Second Printing This Format, 1987
Copyright © 1984, 1977 by General Mills, Inc., Minneapolis, Minnesota.
All rights reserved. Produced in the U.S.A.
Library of Congress Catalog Card Number: 83-82257
Golden®, Golden Press®, and Griffin Design are trademarks of
Western Publishing Company, Inc.
ISBN 0-307-09441-3

It wasn't all that long ago that the microwave was looked upon as something of an "abracadabra" kitchen gadget — a speedy thawer of frozen foods, a quick reheater of yesterday's casserole.

But today, microwave cooking has come of age. And no longer is the microwave considered to be a gimmick, but rather an important, meaningful and, to many, even indispensable appliance. While speed may still be its most obvious asset, it offers many other benefits as well. It's cool — the interior never heats up. It's clean — if food should spatter, it can simply be wiped off with a damp cloth. It's convenient — you can heat and serve in the same utensil, be it a casserole, a plate or a soup mug. It saves energy — and because food is prepared so quickly, little or nothing "cooks away."

It stands to reason, then, that the more you use your microwave, the more you will enjoy its many benefits and the more it will lighten your everyday cooking chores. And that's the purpose of this book. In it you will find the kinds of recipes you've always enjoyed — but especially adapted to the speed and ease of microwaving. So there's no reason to change your menus just to suit a new method of cooking. We think you'll be delighted with the new-found nuances of Sweet 'n Sour Pork and Tuna Shells, with the tender crispness of Orange-buttered Carrots, with the extra-light touch that's brought to Banana-topped Cake. Included, too, are Sugar-baked Apples, Pecan Tarts and other desserts as well as recipes for soups, sandwiches and snacks. And every recipe has been tested in the Betty Crocker Kitchens.

As you use these recipes, we hope you will discover that microwaving is as versatile and exciting as it is clean, cool and quick. Enjoy it . . . and your new-found time.

CONTENTS

THE WHYS AND WHEREFORES

There's more to microwave cooking than pushing a button. And like anything new, it takes some getting used to. Microwave cooking is not just a matter of cooking a faster way; it's cooking in a new and different way. It calls for a certain sense of adventure — a willingness to experiment with your favorite foods and recipes on a trial-and-error basis and to change some of your long-established cooking habits and techniques.

MICROWAVES — HOW THEY WORK

There's nothing magical about microwaves. They are simply electromagnetic waves of energy, very similar to radio and television waves. The magnetron tube converts regular electricity into microwaves. These microwaves, deflected by metal, bounce off the walls, floor and ceiling of the interior in an irregular pattern.

But when they encounter any matter containing moisture — specifically food — they are absorbed into it. (A stirrer fan further deflects the microwaves so that they penetrate the food from all sides.) The microwaves agitate and vibrate the moisture molecules at such a great rate that friction is created; the friction, in turn, creates heat and the heat causes the food to cook. (In conventional cooking methods, heat is applied to the food; with microwaving, heat is generated within the food. Unlike a conventional oven, the microwave never heats up.) Because microwaves only go about 1 inch into

the food, the additional heating or cooking occurs by conduction and/or convection. It is this same conduction that heats the dishes that hold the food—so remember to use hot pads.

UTENSILS

The best utensils for microwave cooking are those that permit the microwaves to pass right through them and into the food. Although there are many specially developed "microwave-suitable" products on the market, chances are you have plenty of utensils on hand.

⦿ Glassware is very well suited to microwave heating and cooking. It's best to use oven-tempered glass for cooking. Cooked food does become very hot, and that heat is transferred to the utensil; thus, the material must be strong enough to withstand high temperatures.

⦿ Dishwasher-safe plastic containers can also be used for quick reheatings. They are not recommended for cooking, however, as the hot food can distort and even melt the plastic. The plastic cooking pouches that contain frozen vegetables and entrées can withstand very high temperatures and may be used successfully in a microwave. Just make a slit in the pouch to allow for the escape of steam.

⦿ Ceramic plates and casseroles are microwave-safe if they contain no metals. However, many varieties of clay and claylike compositions may have traces of metal; so if you are in doubt, test them. To test any dish, place 1 cup water in a glass measure in the microwave on or beside the dish. Microwave 1 minute on the 100% setting. If the dish becomes warm, it should not be used for microwaving.

• China can also be used in the microwave. Just be sure there are no metal decorations or trims to deflect the microwaves.

• Metal utensils should not be used in microwave cooking. Microwaves cannot penetrate metal; rather, they are deflected by it. However, some manufacturers suggest using small pieces of aluminum foil to shield certain areas that might otherwise tend to overcook (for example, the wing tips on a chicken), some even allow the use of TV-dinner trays. Be sure to follow your manufacturer's recommendations to the letter — don't experiment.

WATCH THE TIME

Timing recipes tends to be a little tricky in a microwave — there are more variables than you might expect. When converting a favorite recipe to the microwave method, find a similar recipe in the instruction book that came with your microwave or in this book and use it as your guide. When trying a recipe for the first time, always cook it to the minimum side if a time range is given. If underdone, you can always cook it a bit longer. Why these cautions?

• The density of food has a bearing on the cooking time. Porous foods such as breads and cakes heat or cook very quickly, while dense foods such as roasts and casseroles call for longer cooking times.

• Starting temperatures can also make a difference. The colder the food, the longer the time required to heat or cook it. (For testing the recipes in this book, foods stored at room temperature were used at that temperature, while foods stored in the refrigerator were prepared at that storage temperature.)

• The quantity of food is another factor. For any given microwave setting, there is always the same number of microwaves available for heating or cooking. If only one item is in the cavity, all the microwaves are concentrated on that single item. If there are more items in the cavity, the microwaves must be shared and the concentration on each item is reduced, thus increasing the time required to heat or cook.

TO COVER OR NOT TO COVER

Coverings are often used to keep the moisture in and to prevent liquid foods from spattering. When using the recipes in this book, be aware of the following terminology:

• "Cover" means that no steam or moisture should escape. If using a casserole, use its

---

MICROWAVE POWER

Microwave ovens with variable power control offer a range of settings. Although high (100%) is the most frequently used power level setting, certain foods require a lower setting, or more than one setting, for best results.

POWER LEVEL SETTINGS	PERCENT OF POWER OUTPUT	APPROXIMATE WATTAGE
High	100	550
Medium-High	70	385
Medium	50	275
Medium-Low	30	165
Low	10	55

Check your manufacturer's use and care instructions for the appropriate percent of power needed to be compatible with the recipe instructions in this book.

matching lid or, lacking that, rest a microwave-safe plate on top.

⚫ "Cover tightly" is used in recipes calling for utensils that normally do not have fitted covers. If using a utensil with an odd shape, cover the top with plastic wrap, sealing it all the way around, then turn back one edge slightly.

⚫ "Cover loosely" means that a certain amount of moisture and steam should be permitted to escape from the food. If using a casserole, put the lid on slightly ajar. With other utensils, such as baking dishes, glass measures or bowls, cover with a sheet of waxed paper.

THE SHAPE OF THINGS

Be willing to see things a little differently. In microwave cooking, the more surface that is exposed, the faster and more evenly the food will cook.

⚫ Place thicker pieces of meat toward the sides of the dish, the bonier parts toward the center. Arrange the blossom ends of broccoli in the center, with the stalks radiating out to the sides.

⚫ If heating several items on a plate — sweet rolls for example — arrange them in a circle. And don't place one in the center.

⚫ A circle shape is almost ideal for microwave cooking. It's even better if the circle is a ring, eliminating the slower-to-cook center altogether. This shape is used for many cakelike

desserts as well as for some meat dishes. There are a number of glass, ceramic and plastic ring dishes on the market, but you can improvise by putting a straight-sided beverage glass in the center of a bowl or casserole. The circle shape eliminates corners, which, with certain types of food, tend to overcook because of the heavy concentration of microwaves at the outer edges.

SPECIAL TWISTS

Because the microwaves bounce around the cavity in random patterns, foods often cook faster in one area of the cavity, or even in one area of a baking dish, than in another. Thus it is sometimes necessary to rotate the dish, re-arrange food, stir it or even to let it stand for a while in order to even out the cooking.

⚫ Turn dishes one-quarter or one-half turn midway through the cooking period as directed or when necessary.

⚫ Stirring helps even out the cooking for many sauces and casserolelike dishes. Always stir from the outside edges (where the food is hotter) into the center. Foods that can be stirred usually do not require rotating or standing.

⚫ A "standing time" after cooking allows the heat in the food to equalize. Standing times are also used when a food is heating or cooking more quickly than desired.

IT'S TODAY'S WAY

The recipes on the following pages have been specially chosen to show you how microwave cooking can come to the fore in preparing your daily meals. These are the types of foods you like to prepare for your family; they're the types of foods your family likes to eat.

And while you are exploring the world of microwave cooking, we also hope you will take a tip from our serving recommendations and discover a healthier way of eating. Although these servings may seem small at first glance, each portion has been carefully checked for its protein adequacy.

Speedier cooking. Healthier eating. Two good ideas for today.

NOTE
All the recipes in this book were developed and tested in countertop microwaves with wattage output ratings of 625 to 700 watts. A variety of makes and models with different features and power settings was used. If your microwave has a wattage output of less than 625 watts, you will find that some increase in the suggested cooking time may be required.

MAIN DISHES

BEEF STROGANOFF

1 tablespoon vegetable oil
1 pound boneless beef sirloin steak, cut
    into thin strips
8 ounces fresh mushrooms, sliced
1 medium onion, sliced
¼ cup water
2 tablespoons flour
1 teaspoon dry mustard
1 teaspoon salt
¼ teaspoon pepper
1 cup dairy sour cream
2 cups hot cooked rice or noodles

Stir oil and meat in 2-quart casserole until beef is coated. Cover and microwave on high (100%) until meat is no longer pink, 4½ to 5 minutes. Remove meat from casserole; reserve meat and juices.

Add mushrooms and onion to meat juices. Cover and microwave until mushrooms are tender, 5 to 6 minutes.

Shake water and flour in tightly covered jar; stir into mushrooms. Sprinkle with dry mustard, salt and pepper. Microwave uncovered to boiling, 30 seconds. Boil until thickened, 1 minute.

Stir in reserved meat, then sour cream. Microwave uncovered until hot, about 1 minute. Serve over rice or noodles.

4 servings.

ORIENTAL BEEF AND PEA PODS

1 small head cauliflower
1 green pepper, cut into strips
1 pound beef round steak or tenderloin tip,
    cut into paper-thin strips, about
    3 inches long
1 clove garlic, minced
1 medium onion, chopped
3 tablespoons soy sauce
1 package (6 ounces) frozen pea pods
2 cups water
¼ cup cornstarch
4 teaspoons instant beef bouillon
½ teaspoon sugar
3 cups hot cooked rice

Break cauliflower into flowerets; cut each into ¼-inch slices. Combine cauliflower, green pepper, beef, garlic and onion in 2-quart casserole. Drizzle with soy sauce; stir lightly to coat evenly. Cover and microwave on high (100%) 6 minutes; stir. Cover and microwave until meat is no longer pink, 3 to 5 minutes.

Add frozen pea pods. Cover and microwave until pea pods are thawed, 2 to 3 minutes.

Mix water, cornstarch, bouillon and sugar in 4-cup glass measure. Stir in juices from meat. Microwave uncovered on high (100%) 2½ minutes; stir. Microwave to boiling, 2 to 3 minutes. Stir into meat mixture. Serve over rice.

4 to 6 servings.

PEPPER STEAK STRIPS

1   envelope (about .8 ounce) instant meat
      marinade
1   pound beef round steak, cut into strips,
      about 1/8 inch thick and 3 inches long
1   medium onion, chopped
2   tablespoons margarine or butter
1   teaspoon bottled brown bouquet sauce
1   can (8 ounces) stewed tomatoes
1/2   teaspoon dried thyme leaves
2   tablespoons flour
1/4   cup dry red wine or water
1   medium green pepper, cut into strips
1   can (8 ounces) mushroom stems and
      pieces, drained
3   cups hot cooked rice

Prepare marinade as directed on envelope. Marinate beef as directed on envelope; drain well.

Cover and microwave onion and margarine in 2-quart casserole on high (100%) 1 minute. Stir in bouquet sauce, tomatoes and thyme. Mix in beef. Cover and microwave 8 minutes; stir. Microwave on medium (50%) 10 minutes.

Shake flour and wine in tightly covered container. Stir into meat mixture. Add pepper strips and mushrooms; mix into sauce. Cover and microwave until meat is tender, 6 to 8 minutes. Serve over rice.

5 servings.

TANGY SHORT RIBS

4   pounds beef short ribs, cut into 2-inch
      pieces
3/4   cup lemon juice
1/2   cup steak sauce
1   large onion, sliced
1   clove garlic, finely chopped
2   teaspoons salt
2   teaspoons chili powder
1 1/2   teaspoons ground cumin
1/2   teaspoon pepper

Place beef ribs in 4-quart casserole or bowl. Mix remaining ingredients; pour over ribs. Cover and refrigerate about 1 hour, turning occasionally.

Cover tightly and microwave on medium (50%) until ribs are tender, 1 1/4 to 1 1/2 hours, rearranging ribs every 30 minutes.

4 to 6 servings.

QUICK BEEF STEW

2   to 2 1/2 cups cut-up cooked beef (about
      1 pound)
4   medium carrots, cut into 2 1/2-inch strips
3   medium potatoes, pared and cut into
      1 1/2-inch pieces
1   cup sliced celery
1   envelope (1 3/8 ounces) onion soup mix
3   tablespoons flour
2 1/4   cups water

Mix all ingredients in 2 1/2-quart casserole. Cover and microwave on high (100%) to boiling, 10 to 12 minutes; stir. Cover and let stand 5 minutes. Microwave until vegetables are tender, 10 to 12 minutes, stirring every 5 minutes.

4 to 6 servings.

Pictured at left: Just right for company — Pepper Steak Strips (above) served with piping hot rice.

DRIED BEEF AND NOODLE CASSEROLE

4 ounces dried beef, snipped into small
   pieces
1 cup water
1 small onion, chopped
2 cups uncooked noodles
1 can (10¾ ounces) condensed cream of
   mushroom soup
½ cup milk
1 cup water
1 teaspoon dried parsley flakes
1 cup shredded Cheddar cheese (about
   4 ounces)

Cover and microwave dried beef and 1 cup water in 2-quart casserole on high (100%) to boiling, 2 to 3 minutes; drain.

Stir in onion, noodles, soup, milk, water and parsley flakes. Cover and microwave 10 minutes; stir. Cover and microwave until noodles are tender, 5 to 6 minutes.

Stir in cheese. Cover and microwave until melted, 2 to 3 minutes. Let stand 5 minutes.

5 or 6 servings.

LIVER AND ONIONS

½ pound calf or beef liver, ¼ to ½ inch thick
2 medium onions, sliced
2 tablespoons vegetable oil
¼ teaspoon pepper
¼ teaspoon ground sage
2 teaspoons soy sauce
1 tablespoon lemon juice
   Chopped parsley

Cut liver into serving pieces. Mix onions, oil, pepper and sage in 1-quart casserole. Cover and microwave on high (100%) until onions are crisp-tender, 4 to 6 minutes.

Brush liver with soy sauce. Arrange with thickest pieces to outside in 9-inch pie plate. Spoon onions evenly over liver. Cover tightly and microwave on high (100%) 3 minutes; turn pie plate one-half turn. Microwave until liver is no longer pink, 1 to 3 minutes (do not overcook). Let stand 3 minutes. (Liver will continue to cook while standing.) Sprinkle with lemon juice and parsley.

3 servings.

HAMBURGER PATTIES

1 pound hamburger
1 small onion, chopped
1 slice bread, cubed
2 tablespoons catsup
½ teaspoon salt
1½ teaspoons prepared mustard
1 teaspoon Worcestershire sauce
1 teaspoon prepared horseradish

Mix all ingredients. Shape into 4 patties, about 3½ inches in diameter. Place in square baking dish, 8 x 8 x 2 inches. If desired, brush each patty with additional catsup. Cover loosely and microwave on high (100%) 5 minutes; turn dish one-quarter turn. Microwave until done, 2 to 3 minutes.

4 patties.

Note: Because germs can get mixed into hamburger during preparation, it should be thoroughly cooked, until all trace of pink disappears.

ONION-SESAME HAMBURGERS

    Sesame Topper (below)
1 **pound hamburger**
½ **cup dairy sour cream**
¼ **cup dry bread crumbs**
3 **tablespoons onion soup mix (half of**
    1⅜-ounce envelope)
    Dash of pepper

Prepare Sesame Topper. Mix remaining ingredients. Shape into 4 patties, about ¾ inch thick. Place on microwave roasting rack in baking dish. Cover loosely and microwave on high (100%) 3 minutes; turn dish one-half turn. Microwave until patties are almost done, about 2 minutes. Let stand 3 minutes. Spread Sesame Topper over hamburgers.

4 servings.

SESAME TOPPER
2 **tablespoons margarine or butter,**
    softened
1 **tablespoon toasted sesame seed**
1 **teaspoon Worcestershire sauce**
¼ **teaspoon garlic powder**

Mix all ingredients.

Note: To toast sesame seed, place in 6-ounce custard cup. Microwave uncovered on high (100%) 1 minute; stir. Microwave until toasted, 1 to 3 minutes, watching carefully and stirring every 30 seconds; cool.

ZESTY HAMBURGERS

2 **tablespoons margarine or butter**
1 **teaspoon Worcestershire sauce**
¼ **teaspoon lemon juice**
1 **clove garlic, minced**
1 **small onion, sliced**
1 **cup sliced fresh mushrooms**
1 **pound lean hamburger**
½ **teaspoon salt**
¼ **teaspoon pepper**

Microwave margarine uncovered in 4-cup glass measure on high (100%) until melted, 30 seconds to 1 minute. Stir in Worcestershire sauce, lemon juice, garlic, onion and mushrooms. Cover loosely and microwave until onion is crisp-tender, about 2 minutes.

Mix hamburger, salt and pepper. Shape into 4 patties, about ¾ inch thick. Place in square baking dish, 8 x 8 x 2 inches. Cover loosely and microwave on high (100%) until almost done, 6 to 7 minutes; drain. Spoon mushroom mixture onto hamburgers. Cover and microwave until hot, about 1 minute.

4 servings.

VEGETABLE-FILLED PATTIES

1 **pound lean hamburger**
⅔ **cup dry bread crumbs**
¼ **cup finely chopped onion**
1 **egg**
1 **teaspoon salt**
⅛ **teaspoon pepper**
1 **can (10¾ ounces) condensed cream of**
    mushroom soup
½ **can (2.8-ounce size) French fried onions**
1 **can (16 ounces) French-style green**
    beans, drained
½ **teaspoon Worcestershire sauce**

Mix hamburger, bread crumbs, chopped onion, egg, salt, pepper and ⅓ cup of the soup. Shape into 6 oval patties. Place in oblong baking dish, 12 x 7½ x 2 inches. Depress center of each patty, forming a ½-inch rim around edge.

Reserve a few French fried onions for garnish. Mix remaining onions with beans, Worcestershire sauce and remaining soup; spoon into center of each patty. Cover loosely and microwave on high (100%) 6 minutes; turn dish one-half turn. Microwave until meat is done, 6 to 8 minutes. Garnish with reserved onions.

6 servings.

HAWAIIAN MEATBALLS

  1 **pound hamburger**
 ½ **cup dry bread crumbs**
  1 **tablespoon instant minced onion**
 ⅛ **teaspoon pepper**
  1 **egg**
 ¼ **cup milk**
  1 **tablespoon soy sauce**
 ½ **cup packed brown sugar**
 ¼ **cup all-purpose flour**
  2 **tablespoons soy sauce**
  8 **green onions, cut into 1-inch pieces**
  1 **clove garlic, crushed**
  1 **can (20 ounces) pineapple chunks**
  1 **green pepper, cut into 1-inch pieces**

Mix hamburger, bread crumbs, onion, pepper, egg, milk and 1 tablespoon soy sauce. Shape into meatballs, about 1½ inches in diameter. Place in 3-quart casserole. Cover loosely and microwave on high (100%) 3 minutes; rearrange meatballs. Cover and microwave until meatballs are done, 5 to 7 minutes. Let stand 3 minutes. Remove meatballs; drain fat from casserole.

Mix brown sugar and flour in casserole. Stir in 2 tablespoons soy sauce, the onions, garlic and pineapple (with syrup). Microwave uncovered on high (100%) 2 minutes; stir. Microwave until mixture boils and thickens, 3 to 4 minutes. Stir in meatballs and green pepper. Cover and microwave until pepper is crisp-tender, 3 to 4 minutes. Serve with Green Beans and Bamboo Shoots if desired.

5 or 6 servings.

A touch of the exotic: Hawaiian Meatballs (above) and Green Beans and Bamboo Shoots (page 49)

MEATBALLS

1 pound hamburger
1 small onion, chopped
2 slices bread, cubed
1 egg
¼ cup milk
1 teaspoon salt
1 teaspoon Worcestershire sauce
⅛ teaspoon pepper

Mix all ingredients. Shape into 12 meatballs, about 2 inches in diameter. Place in baking dish, 8 x 8 x 2 inches. Cover loosely and microwave on high (100%) 4 minutes; rearrange meatballs. Cover and microwave until meatballs are done, 3 to 4 minutes; drain.

12 meatballs.

SWEET-SOUR MEATBALLS

Meatballs (above)
2 tablespoons cornstarch
1 can (15¼ ounces) pineapple chunks
½ cup chopped green pepper
½ cup packed brown sugar
¼ cup vinegar
1 tablespoon soy sauce

Prepare and microwave Meatballs. Mix cornstarch and pineapple (with syrup) in 4-cup glass measure. Stir in green pepper, brown sugar, vinegar and soy sauce. Microwave uncovered on high (100%) 2 minutes; stir. Microwave to boiling, 1½ minutes. Boil until thickened and translucent, 2½ to 3½ minutes.

Pour sauce over meatballs. Microwave uncovered on high (100%) until meatballs are hot, 4 to 5 minutes.

4 to 6 servings.

SPANISH MEAT LOAF

1½ pounds hamburger
1 cup dry bread crumbs
⅔ cup milk
⅓ cup tomato sauce
1 egg
1 small onion, chopped
1 tablespoon Worcestershire sauce
1½ teaspoons salt
½ teaspoon dry mustard
¼ teaspoon pepper
¼ teaspoon ground sage
8 large pimiento-stuffed olives, sliced
1 clove garlic, crushed (optional)
⅔ cup tomato sauce

Mix all ingredients except ⅔ cup tomato sauce. Press into 2-quart casserole. Spread ⅔ cup tomato sauce over meat. Cover and microwave on high (100%) 7 minutes; turn casserole one-quarter turn. Microwave until done, 8 to 10 minutes. Let stand 5 minutes before cutting.

6 servings.

FAMILY MEAT LOAF

1½ cups herb-seasoned stuffing mix
⅔ cup milk
1½ pounds hamburger
1 small onion, chopped
1 egg
1 teaspoon salt
¼ teaspoon pepper

Pour milk over stuffing cubes. Mix in remaining ingredients. Press evenly into loaf dish, 9 x 5 x 3 inches. Cover loosely and microwave on high (100%) 10 minutes; turn loaf dish one-half turn. Microwave until meat is set in center, 5 to 6 minutes.

4 to 6 servings.

CHEESE-FILLED MEAT LOAF

  1 **pound lean hamburger**
⅔ **cup dry bread crumbs**
  1 **can (10½ ounces) pizza sauce**
  1 **egg**
  1 **medium onion, chopped**
  1 **teaspoon salt**
⅛ **teaspoon garlic powder**
  1 **carton (12 ounces) small curd cottage cheese**
  1 **can (4 ounces) mushroom stems and pieces, drained**
  1 **tablespoon dried parsley flakes**
¾ **teaspoon Italian seasoning**
  1 **egg**

Mix hamburger, bread crumbs, ½ cup of the pizza sauce, 1 egg, the onion, salt and garlic powder; reserve. Mix remaining ingredients for cheese filling.

Press ⅓ of the meat mixture in bottom of oblong baking dish, 10 x 6 x 1½ inches. Spread cheese filling over meat. Spoon remaining meat mixture onto top; spread to cover filling. Cover loosely and microwave on high (100%) 10 minutes; turn dish one-quarter turn. Microwave until meat is firm in center, about 7 minutes. Let stand 5 minutes before cutting.

Microwave remaining pizza sauce uncovered in dish to boiling, 1 to 2 minutes; serve over meat loaf.

8 servings.

TEXAS HASH

  1 **pound hamburger**
  3 **large onions, sliced**
  1 **large green pepper, chopped**
  1 **can (16 ounces) whole tomatoes**
¾ **cup instant rice**
  2 **teaspoons salt**
  1 **to 2 teaspoons chili powder**
⅛ **teaspoon pepper**

Crumble hamburger into 3-quart casserole; add onions and green pepper. Cover and microwave on high (100%) 4 minutes. Stir to break up meat. Cover and microwave until vegetables are tender, 4 to 6 minutes; drain.

Stir in tomatoes (with liquid), rice, salt, chili powder and pepper. Cover and microwave 5 minutes; stir. Cover and microwave until rice is almost tender, 4 to 6 minutes. Let stand 5 minutes.

6 servings.

HEARTY BEEF CASSEROLE

1½ **pounds hamburger**
  1 **large onion, chopped**
  2 **medium tomatoes, chopped**
  2 **cups water**
  1 **cup uncooked bulgur wheat**
  3 **tablespoons chopped parsley**
  2 **teaspoons instant beef bouillon**
1½ **teaspoons salt**
½ **teaspoon dried oregano leaves**
¼ **teaspoon instant minced garlic**
¼ **teaspoon pepper**
½ **cup grated Parmesan cheese**

Crumble hamburger into 3-quart casserole; add onion. Cover loosely and microwave on high (100%) 5 minutes; stir. Cover and microwave until meat is firm, 4 to 6 minutes. Stir to break up meat; drain.

Stir in remaining ingredients except cheese. Cover and microwave 10 minutes; stir. Cover and microwave until wheat is tender, 10 to 14 minutes. Stir in cheese. Sprinkle with additional Parmesan cheese and chopped parsley if desired.

7 servings.

CREAMY HAMBURGER-NOODLE HOT DISH

1 pound hamburger
1 medium onion, chopped
1 clove garlic, minced
2½ cups uncooked noodles
2 teaspoons instant beef bouillon
½ teaspoon dry mustard
½ teaspoon salt
  Dash of pepper
1 can (4 ounces) mushroom stems and
    pieces
¼ cup dry white wine or water
2 tablespoons tomato paste
2 cups water
¾ cup dairy sour cream

Crumble hamburger into 2-quart casserole; add onion and garlic. Microwave uncovered on high (100%) until meat is firm, 5 to 6 minutes. Stir to break up meat; drain.

Stir in noodles, bouillon, mustard, salt, pepper, mushrooms (with liquid), wine, tomato paste and water. Cover and microwave until mixture boils and noodles are tender, 11 to 13 minutes, stirring every 4 minutes. Stir in sour cream. Let stand uncovered 5 minutes.

4 to 6 servings.

UPSIDE-DOWN MEAT PIE

1 pound hamburger
½ cup chopped celery
1 medium onion, chopped
1 can (10¾ ounces) condensed tomato
    soup
1 teaspoon Worcestershire sauce
½ teaspoon salt
⅛ teaspoon pepper
2 eggs
½ package (10-ounce size) frozen peas
    (1 cup)
1½ cups buttermilk baking mix
½ cup water
¼ cup grated Parmesan cheese or
    shredded process cheese
  Paprika

Crumble hamburger into 2-quart casserole, about 9 inches in diameter; add celery and onion. Microwave uncovered on high (100%) until meat is firm, 5 to 6 minutes. Stir to break up meat; drain.

Stir in soup, Worcestershire sauce, salt, pepper, eggs and frozen peas. Cover and microwave 5 minutes; stir. Microwave uncovered until hot and bubbly, 3 minutes.

Mix baking mix, water and cheese. Spoon onto hot meat mixture, spreading to cover. Sprinkle with paprika. Microwave uncovered 3 minutes; turn casserole one-quarter turn. Microwave until topping is no longer doughy, 2 to 3 minutes. Spoon or invert onto serving plate and cut into wedges.

5 or 6 servings.

◀ Place filled green peppers in baking dish and cover loosely. "Cover loosely" means that some steam and moisture should be allowed to escape from the food. Here, plastic wrap is used as the covering, but the corners have been turned back.

▶ Use a glass measure to microwave sauces — measure, mix and microwave in one utensil.

Quick and easy: Top Hat Stuffed Peppers

TOP HAT STUFFED PEPPERS

- 5 green peppers
- 1 pound hamburger
- ¼ cup chopped celery
- 1 cup instant rice
- ⅓ cup catsup
- 2 tablespoons chopped onion
- 1 tablespoon Worcestershire sauce
- ½ teaspoon salt
- ⅛ teaspoon garlic powder
-    Dash of pepper
- 1 egg
- 1 can (8 ounces) tomato sauce
- 1 teaspoon sugar
- ¼ teaspoon dried basil leaves

Cut thin slice from stem end of each pepper. Remove all seeds and membranes; wash inside and out.

Mix hamburger, celery, rice, catsup, onion, Worcestershire sauce, salt, garlic powder, pepper and egg. Fill peppers with meat mixture. Place in square baking dish, 8 x 8 x 2 inches. Cover loosely and microwave on high (100%) until meat is firm, 10 to 12 minutes.

Mix tomato sauce, sugar and basil in 2-cup glass measure. Microwave uncovered on high (100%) to boiling, 2 to 3 minutes. Serve sauce over peppers.

5 servings.

STUFFED CABBAGE ROLLS

- 12 cabbage leaves
- ¼ cup cold water
- 1 pound lean hamburger
- ½ cup instant rice
- 1 medium onion, chopped
- 1 can (4 ounces) mushroom stems and pieces
- 1 teaspoon salt
- ⅛ teaspoon garlic salt
- ⅛ teaspoon pepper
- 1 can (15 ounces) tomato sauce
- 1 teaspoon sugar
- ½ teaspoon lemon juice
- 1 tablespoon cornstarch
- 1 tablespoon cold water

Cover and microwave cabbage leaves and ¼ cup cold water in 3-quart casserole on high (100%) until limp, 4 to 5 minutes; drain.

Mix hamburger, rice, onion, mushrooms (with liquid), salt, garlic salt, pepper and ½ cup of the tomato sauce. Place about ⅓ cup meat mixture at stem end of each cabbage leaf. Roll leaf around meat mixture, tucking in sides. Place cabbage rolls seam sides down in 3-quart casserole.

Mix remaining tomato sauce, the sugar and lemon juice. Blend cornstarch and 1 tablespoon water; stir into tomato sauce mixture. Pour over cabbage rolls. Cover and microwave on high (100%) 7 minutes; turn casserole one-quarter turn. Microwave until meat is done, 8 to 9 minutes. Let stand 1 minute. Remove cabbage rolls to platter. Stir sauce in casserole with fork; pour over cabbage rolls.

4 to 6 servings.

Note: To separate leaves from cabbage head, remove core and cover cabbage with cold water. Let stand about 10 minutes; remove leaves.

ONE-DISH SPAGHETTI CASSEROLE

    1   pound hamburger
    1   medium onion, chopped
    ½   cup chopped celery
    1   can (28 ounces) whole tomatoes
    1   can (4 ounces) mushroom stems and
          pieces, drained
 1½   cups water
    1   teaspoon salt
    ½   teaspoon garlic salt
    1   package (7 ounces) thin spaghetti,
          broken into 3-inch pieces
        Grated Parmesan cheese (optional)

Crumble hamburger into 3-quart casserole; add onion and celery. Microwave uncovered on high (100%) until meat is firm, 5 to 6 minutes. Stir to break up meat; drain.

Stir tomatoes (with liquid), mushrooms, water and salts into meat mixture. Cover and microwave 5 minutes.

Stir in spaghetti. Cover and microwave until spaghetti is tender, 15 to 17 minutes, stirring every 5 minutes. Let stand 5 minutes. Sprinkle with cheese.

6 servings.

IMPOSSIBLE CHEESEBURGER PIE

    1   pound hamburger
    3   medium onions, chopped
    ½   teaspoon salt
    ¼   teaspoon pepper
 1½   cups milk
    3   eggs
    ¾   cup buttermilk baking mix
    2   tomatoes, sliced
    1   cup shredded Cheddar or process
          American cheese (about 4 ounces)

Crumble hamburger into 10-inch pie plate; add onions. Cover loosely and microwave on high (100%) 3 minutes; stir. Cover and microwave until meat is firm, 3 to 4 minutes. Stir to break

up meat; drain. Stir in salt and pepper. Beat milk, eggs and baking mix until smooth, 15 seconds in blender on high or 1 minute with hand beater. Pour over meat mixture.

Microwave uncovered on medium-high (70%) until knife inserted in center comes out clean, 12 to 18 minutes, turning pie plate one-quarter turn every 6 minutes. Top with tomatoes and cheese. Microwave until cheese is almost melted, 6 to 8 minutes, turning pie plate one-quarter turn every 3 minutes. Let stand 5 minutes.

6 to 8 servings.

HAMBURGER PIE ITALIANO

    1   pound hamburger
    1   egg
    2   tablespoons dry bread crumbs
    1   teaspoon salt
    1   teaspoon Italian seasoning
    ¼   teaspoon pepper
    1   can (6 ounces) tomato paste
    1   small green pepper, sliced
    1   cup shredded mozzarella cheese
          (about 4 ounces)
    1   teaspoon dried oregano leaves

Crumble hamburger into 1-quart casserole. Microwave uncovered on high (100%) 3 minutes; stir. Microwave until meat is firm, 2 to 3 minutes. Stir to break up meat finely; drain.

Stir in egg, bread crumbs, salt, Italian seasoning and pepper. Press in bottom and up side of 9-inch pie plate. Microwave uncovered on high (100%) until meat is set, 4½ to 5½ minutes.

Spread tomato paste over meat; top with green pepper, cheese and oregano. Microwave uncovered until cheese is melted, 2 to 3 minutes. Cut into wedges.

5 or 6 servings.

BEEF AND BEANS
WITH CORN BREAD TOPPING

¾ pound hamburger
 1 medium onion, chopped
 1 can (16 ounces) pork and beans in
     tomato sauce
½ cup barbecue sauce
½ teaspoon salt
     Corn Bread Topping (below)

Crumble hamburger into 2-quart casserole; add onion. Microwave uncovered on high (100%) until meat is firm, 5 to 6 minutes. Stir to break up meat; drain.

Stir in pork and beans, barbecue sauce and salt. Cover and microwave to boiling, 3 to 4 minutes.

Prepare Corn Bread Topping. Spoon onto meat mixture, forming a ring of corn bread around side of casserole. (Topping will cook toward center.) Microwave uncovered 2 minutes; turn casserole one-quarter turn. Microwave until topping is no longer doughy, 2 to 3 minutes.

5 servings.

CORN BREAD TOPPING
½ cup buttermilk baking mix
¼ cup yellow cornmeal
 2 teaspoons sugar
⅛ teaspoon salt
 2 teaspoons vegetable oil
 1 egg, slightly beaten
¼ cup milk

Mix all ingredients until well blended.

BEEF ENCHILADAS

 1 pound hamburger
 1 medium onion, chopped
 1 cup shredded Cheddar cheese (about
     4 ounces)
½ cup dairy sour cream
 2 tablespoons chopped parsley
 1 teaspoon salt
¼ teaspoon pepper
 8 nine-inch tortillas
     Tomato Sauce (below)

Crumble hamburger into 2-quart casserole; add onion. Cover loosely and microwave on high (100%) 3 minutes; stir. Cover and microwave until meat is firm, 2 to 3 minutes. Stir to break up meat; drain. Stir in cheese, sour cream, parsley, salt and pepper. Cover and reserve.

Wrap 4 tortillas in damp cloth and microwave on high (100%) until softened, about 45 seconds. (Keep tortillas covered while working with filling.) Spoon about ⅓ cup meat mixture in center of tortilla. Fold sides of tortilla up over filling, overlapping edges. Place tortilla seam side down in oblong baking dish, 12 x 7½ x 2 inches. Repeat with remaining tortillas.

Prepare Tomato Sauce. Pour sauce over tortillas. Cover loosely and microwave on high (100%) until filling is hot, 7 to 9 minutes. Garnish with slices of ripe olives, avocado, hardcooked egg or shredded cheese if desired.

4 or 5 servings.

TOMATO SAUCE
 1 can (15 ounces) tomato sauce
⅓ cup water
⅓ cup chopped green pepper
 1 clove garlic, finely chopped
1½ to 2 teaspoons chili powder
½ teaspoon dried oregano leaves
¼ teaspoon ground cumin

Mix all ingredients in 4-cup glass measure. Cover tightly and microwave on high (100%) to boiling, 4 to 6 minutes; stir.

MEXICAN PIZZA

1 tablespoon yellow cornmeal
1 cup buttermilk baking mix
¼ cup yellow cornmeal
2 tablespoons margarine or butter, softened
3 tablespoons very hot water
½ pound hamburger
1 jar (8 ounces) taco sauce
¼ cup sliced ripe olives
2 tablespoons drained chopped green chilies
2 tablespoons sliced green onions
½ cup shredded Monterey Jack cheese (about 2 ounces)
½ cup shredded Cheddar cheese (about 2 ounces)

Grease 12-inch glass pizza plate; sprinkle evenly with 1 tablespoon cornmeal. Mix baking mix, ¼ cup cornmeal and the margarine; stir in water until a stiff dough forms. Roll into 12-inch circle on cloth-covered board well floured with baking mix. Place on pizza plate. Pinch edge to form ½-inch rim.

Microwave uncovered on inverted plate on high (100%) 4 minutes; turn pizza plate one-half turn. Microwave until surface is dry, 2 to 4 minutes.

Crumble hamburger into 1-quart casserole. Cover loosely and microwave on high (100%) 2 minutes; stir. Cover and microwave until meat is firm, 1 to 2 minutes. Stir to break up meat; drain.

Cover loosely and microwave taco sauce in 2-cup glass measure on high (100%) until hot, about 2 minutes. Spread sauce over crust; top with meat and remaining ingredients. Microwave uncovered on high (100%) until cheese is melted and bubbly, 3 to 4 minutes.

6 servings.

Family favorite with a twist: Mexican Pizza

ENCHILADA CASSEROLE

1 pound hamburger
1 medium onion, chopped
1 green pepper, chopped
1 can (8 ounces) tomato sauce
1 can (10 ounces) enchilada sauce
1 can (15 ounces) pinto beans
6 six-inch tortillas
1 medium tomato, chopped
½ cup shredded Cheddar cheese (about
    2 ounces)

Crumble hamburger into 1½-quart casserole; add onion and green pepper. Microwave uncovered on high (100%) until meat is firm, 5 to 6 minutes. Stir to break up meat; drain.

Stir in tomato sauce, enchilada sauce and beans (with liquid). Cover and microwave to boiling, 3 to 4½ minutes.

Spoon 2 cups meat sauce into oblong baking dish, 12 x 7½ x 2 inches. Place ¼ cup remaining meat sauce in center of tortilla. Fold sides of tortilla up over filling, overlapping edges. Place tortilla seam side down in baking dish. Repeat with remaining tortillas. Spoon remaining sauce over tortillas. Cover loosely and microwave on high (100%) until hot, 9 to 10 minutes.

Sprinkle tomato in strip down center of baking dish; sprinkle cheese on each side. Microwave uncovered until cheese is melted, 2 to 3 minutes.

6 servings.

PORK TENDERLOIN AND PEPPERS

½ teaspoon dried rosemary leaves
½ teaspoon dried thyme leaves
3 cloves garlic, crushed
1 tablespoon plus 1½ teaspoons
    pork-flavored gravy mix
    (half of .8-ounce envelope)
1 tablespoon vegetable oil
1 fresh pork tenderloin (10 to 12 ounces)
1 medium green pepper, cut into ½-inch
    strips
1 medium red pepper, cut into ½-inch
    strips

Mix rosemary, thyme and garlic until herbs are crushed. Stir in gravy mix and oil. Rub tenderloin with herb mixture.

Place tenderloin in 16 x 10-inch cooking bag. Close bag loosely with string (leave hole the size of finger in closure). Place tenderloin on microwave roasting rack in oblong baking dish, 12 x 7½ x 2 inches.

Microwave on medium-low (30%) 5 minutes; turn dish one-quarter turn. Microwave 5 minutes; turn tenderloin over. Microwave 5 minutes longer; turn tenderloin over. Open bag and place peppers in bag with tenderloin. Close bag loosely and microwave 5 minutes; turn dish one-quarter turn. Microwave until tenderloin is done (170° on meat thermometer in several places), 5 to 8 minutes. To serve, cut tenderloin diagonally into ¼-inch slices. Pour cooking juices over peppers; serve with tenderloin.

3 or 4 servings.

GLAZED PORK LOIN ROAST

2- to 2½-pound boneless fresh pork loin
   roast
1 clove garlic, cut into fourths
1 teaspoon salt
1 tablespoon orange marmalade
1 teaspoon prepared mustard
½ teaspoon dried thyme leaves

Make 4 slits in fat on pork roast with tip of sharp knife; insert a piece of garlic in each slit. Sprinkle roast with salt. Mix marmalade, mustard and thyme; spread on roast.

Place roast in 16 x 10-inch cooking bag. Close bag loosely with string (leave hole the size of finger in closure). Place roast on microwave roasting rack in oblong baking dish, 12 x 7½ x 2 inches.

Microwave on medium-low (30%) 30 minutes; turn roast over and turn dish one-half turn. Microwave until roast is done (170° on meat thermometer in several places), 20 to 25 minutes. Let stand 10 minutes in bag in microwave. Serve with meat juices.

8 to 10 servings.

SWEET 'N SOUR PORK

1½ pounds boneless fresh pork shoulder,
   cut into ½-inch cubes
1 medium onion, sliced
1 can (8 ounces) pineapple chunks
¼ cup packed brown sugar
3 tablespoons cornstarch
2 tablespoons lemon juice
1 tablespoon soy sauce
1 teaspoon salt
⅛ teaspoon pepper
⅛ teaspoon ground ginger
1 small green pepper, cut into 1-inch
   pieces
1 package (6 ounces) frozen pea pods

Mix pork, onion, pineapple (with juice), brown sugar, cornstarch, lemon juice, soy sauce, salt, pepper and ginger in 2-quart casserole. Cover

and microwave on medium (50%) until pork is no longer pink, 24 to 28 minutes, stirring every 3 minutes.

Stir in green pepper and pea pods. Cover and microwave on high (100%) 2 minutes; stir. Cover and microwave until green pepper and pea pods are tender, 3 to 4 minutes.

6 servings.

ORIENTAL PORK

1 pound boneless fresh pork shoulder, cut
   into ¼-inch strips
½ cup water
½ cup orange juice
¼ teaspoon salt
⅛ teaspoon pepper
3 tablespoons soy sauce
1 can (8 ounces) sliced water chestnuts,
   drained
1 can (16 ounces) bean sprouts, drained
2 cups thinly sliced Chinese cabbage
1 tablespoon cornstarch
1 tablespoon cold water
2 tablespoons chopped green onions
3 cups hot cooked rice

Mix pork, ½ cup water, the orange juice, salt, pepper and soy sauce in 2-quart casserole. Cover and microwave on medium (50%) until pork is tender, 16 to 20 minutes, stirring every 3 minutes.

Stir in water chestnuts, bean sprouts and cabbage. Cover and microwave on high (100%) until cabbage is crisp-tender, 3 to 4 minutes.

Blend cornstarch and 1 tablespoon water in 4-cup glass measure. Drain juices from meat mixture into cornstarch mixture; stir well. Microwave uncovered on high (100%) until mixture boils and thickens, 3 to 4 minutes, stirring every minute. Pour over meat and vegetables. Sprinkle with onions. Serve over rice.

4 servings.

PORK WITH VEGETABLES AND CASHEWS

1 pound boneless fresh pork shoulder, cut into ¾-inch cubes
1 medium onion, sliced and separated into rings
2 tablespoons soy sauce
½ teaspoon salt
¼ teaspoon pepper
1 package (10 ounces) frozen peas
8 ounces fresh mushrooms, sliced
1 tablespoon cornstarch
2 tablespoons cold water
1 jar (2 ounces) sliced pimiento, drained
1 cup salted cashews or peanuts

Mix pork, onion and soy sauce in 3-quart casserole. Cover and microwave on medium (50%) until meat is no longer pink, 12 to 15 minutes, stirring every 3 minutes.

Stir in salt, pepper, peas and mushrooms. Cover and microwave on medium (50%) 9 minutes, stirring every 3 minutes.

Blend cornstarch and water; stir into meat mixture. Stir in pimiento. Cover and microwave on medium (50%) until meat is tender, 9 to 12 minutes, stirring every 3 minutes. Stir in cashews. Cover and let stand 5 minutes. Serve with rice if desired.

4 servings.

ITALIAN PORK CHOP BAKE

1 jar (15½ ounces) spaghetti sauce
1¼ cups water
¾ cup long-grain rice
1½ teaspoons salt
⅛ teaspoon pepper
1 can (2.2 ounces) sliced ripe olives, drained
1 small onion, sliced
6 fresh pork loin chops (about 2 pounds), about ½ inch thick

Mix all ingredients except pork chops in oblong baking dish, 12 x 7½ x 2 inches. Cover tightly and microwave on high (100%) 8 to 10 minutes; stir.

Arrange chops in dish with narrow ends toward center, pushing them into sauce. Cover tightly and microwave on medium (50%) 10 minutes; turn dish one-quarter turn. Microwave 10 minutes. Turn and rearrange chops; stir rice. Cover and microwave on medium (50%) until chops and rice are done (170° on meat thermometer), 25 to 35 minutes, turning dish one-quarter turn every 5 minutes. Let stand 10 minutes.

6 servings.

PORK CHOPS WITH APRICOT GLAZE

4 fresh pork loin chops (about 1½ pounds), about ½ inch thick
½ teaspoon salt
½ cup sliced green onions
½ cup apricot preserves
¼ cup dry red wine
1 teaspoon ground ginger
2 teaspoons cornstarch
1 tablespoon cold water
8 canned apricot halves
   Parsley

Arrange pork chops with narrow ends toward center in square baking dish, 8 x 8 x 2 inches. Sprinkle chops with salt and onions. Mix apricot preserves, wine and ginger; pour over chops. Cover tightly and microwave on medium (50%) until chops are done (170° on meat thermometer), 28 to 32 minutes, turning dish one-quarter turn every 5 minutes.

Remove pork chops to serving platter; cover and keep warm. Pour 1 cup of the juices from dish into 2-cup glass measure. Blend cornstarch and water; stir into juices. Microwave uncovered on high (100%) until mixture boils and thickens, 1 to 2 minutes. Spoon sauce over chops. Garnish with apricot halves and parsley. Serve with hot buttered noodles if desired.

4 servings.

PORK CHOPS WITH CRANBERRY RELISH

1 can (8 ounces) jellied cranberry sauce
1 orange (pulp and peel), finely chopped
½ cup golden raisins
2 tablespoons crystallized ginger, finely chopped
 Seasoned Crumbs (below)
4 fresh pork rib or loin chops (about 1½ pounds), about ½ inch thick
¼ cup milk

Cover and microwave cranberry sauce in 1-quart casserole on high (100%) 2 minutes. Stir in orange, raisins and ginger. Cover and microwave until hot and bubbly, 2½ to 3½ minutes. Refrigerate at least 2 hours.

Prepare Seasoned Crumbs. Dip pork chops into milk; shake each in Seasoned Crumbs to coat. Arrange chops with narrow ends toward center on microwave roasting rack in oblong baking dish, 12 x 7½ x 2 inches. Cover loosely and microwave on medium-high (70%) 7 minutes; turn dish one-half turn. Microwave uncovered until chops are done (170° on meat thermometer), 6 to 8 minutes. Serve with cranberry relish.

4 servings.

SEASONED CRUMBS
⅓ cup crushed soda or cocktail cracker crumbs
1 teaspoon ground sage
½ teaspoon salt
½ teaspoon onion powder
½ teaspoon paprika

Mix all ingredients in plastic bag.

BARBECUED RIBS AND PEACHES

2½ to 3 pounds fresh pork country-style ribs, cut into serving pieces
1 teaspoon salt
⅓ teaspoon pepper
1 can (16 ounces) sliced peaches
2 teaspoons cornstarch
¼ cup chili sauce
¼ teaspoon garlic powder

Sprinkle ribs with salt and pepper. Arrange in oblong baking dish, 12 x 7½ x 2 inches. Cover tightly and microwave on medium (50%) until ribs are no longer pink, 25 to 30 minutes, turning dish one-quarter turn every 5 minutes; drain. Rearrange ribs.

Drain peaches, reserving ⅓ cup syrup. Mix reserved peach syrup, the cornstarch, chili sauce and garlic powder; spoon onto ribs. Cover loosely and microwave on medium (50%) until ribs are done (170° on meat thermometer), 30 to 35 minutes, rearranging ribs every 10 minutes. Spoon peaches around ribs. Cover and microwave on high (100%) until hot, 2 to 3 minutes.

6 servings.

Pictured at right: A medley of main dishes — Oriental Beef and Pea Pods (page 7), Barbecued Ribs and Peaches (above) and Mexican-style Egg Cups (page 40)

COUNTRY SPARERIBS WITH WINE SAUCE

   3   pounds fresh pork country-style ribs,
        cut into serving pieces
   1   cup sweet red wine
   ½   cup chili sauce
   ⅓   cup vinegar
   ¼   cup honey
   3   tablespoons soy sauce
   2   teaspoons dry mustard
   1   teaspoon salt
   1   teaspoon prepared horseradish
   1   teaspoon red pepper sauce
   ½   teaspoon pepper
   ½   teaspoon paprika

Place ribs meaty sides up in 3-quart casserole. Cover loosely and microwave on medium (50%) until ribs are no longer pink, 27 to 29 minutes, rearranging ribs every 3 minutes; drain. Rearrange ribs.

Mix remaining ingredients in 4-cup glass measure. Microwave uncovered on high (100%) 2 minutes; stir. Microwave to boiling, 2 to 3 minutes. Pour over ribs. Cover and microwave on medium (50%) 30 minutes; rearrange ribs. Cover and microwave until meat separates from bones, 30 to 45 minutes. Remove ribs to serving bowl; keep warm. Skim fat from sauce; pour sauce over ribs.

5 or 6 servings.

GLAZED HAM PATTIES

   1   pound ground fully cooked ham (about
        3 cups)
   1   egg
   ¼   cup dry bread crumbs
   1   tablespoon finely chopped onion
   2   tablespoons milk
   2   teaspoons dried parsley flakes
   1   teaspoon prepared mustard
   2   tablespoons packed brown sugar
   2   tablespoons honey
   1   teaspoon vinegar
   ⅛   teaspoon ground cloves
   1   tablespoon orange juice

Mix ham, egg, bread crumbs, onion, milk, parsley flakes and mustard. Shape into 4 patties, about 3½ inches in diameter. Place in square baking dish, 8 x 8 x 2 inches.

Mix brown sugar, honey, vinegar and cloves; spread half of the mixture over patties. Stir orange juice into remaining mixture; reserve.

Cover patties loosely and microwave on high (100%) 4 minutes; turn dish one-quarter turn. Microwave until patties are firm in center, 3 to 4 minutes. Serve reserved glaze over patties.

4 servings.

MICROWAVE TIP

Special instant-read thermometers can be used for determining doneness when microwaving meat or fish. Regular mercury-type thermometers should not be used in the microwave. To check the internal temperature of a food, first remove it from the microwave and then check the temperature with an instant-read thermometer. Be sure to remove the thermometer if additional microwaving is necessary.

HAM-PINEAPPLE HAWAIIAN

- 1 cup ¼-inch diagonally sliced carrots
- 1 cup ¼-inch diagonally sliced celery
- ¼ cup water
- 2 cups ½-inch pieces fully cooked smoked ham
- 1 can (8 ounces) pineapple chunks in juice, drained (reserve juice)
- 1 tablespoon margarine or butter
- 2 green onions, diagonally cut into 1-inch pieces
- 1 teaspoon crushed gingerroot
- 1 clove garlic, crushed
- ¼ cup margarine or butter
- 1 tablespoon plus 1½ teaspoons cornstarch
- 1 tablespoon soy sauce
- ⅛ teaspoon pepper
- 2 tablespoons chopped parsley
- 4 cups hot cooked rice

Cover and microwave carrots, celery and water in 1½-quart casserole on high (100%) until crisp-tender, 3 to 5 minutes; drain and reserve.

Mix ham, pineapple, 1 tablespoon margarine, the onions, gingerroot and garlic in 1-quart casserole. Cover and microwave on high (100%) until hot, 4 to 5 minutes, stirring once.

Microwave ¼ cup margarine uncovered in 4-cup glass measure on high (100%) until melted, 30 seconds to 1 minute. Stir in cornstarch and soy sauce until smooth. Add enough water to reserved pineapple juice to measure 1 cup; gradually stir into cornstarch mixture. Stir in pepper. Microwave until mixture boils and thickens, 3 to 4 minutes, stirring every minute.

Mix ham mixture and thickened pineapple juice into carrots and celery. Cover and microwave on medium-high (70%) 4 minutes; turn casserole one-half turn. Microwave until hot, 2 to 4 minutes. Sprinkle with parsley. Serve over rice.

6 servings.

HERB-GLAZED LAMB CHOPS

- 2 or 3 lamb shoulder or leg chops (¾ to 1 pound), about ½ inch thick
- ½ cup water
- 1 tablespoon cornstarch
- 1 teaspoon soy sauce
- ½ teaspoon sugar
- ¼ teaspoon salt
- ¼ teaspoon dried basil leaves
- ⅛ teaspoon dry mustard

Cover and microwave lamb chops in square baking dish, 8 x 8 x 2 inches, on high (100%) 3 minutes; turn chops. Cover and microwave until no longer pink, 2 to 2½ minutes.

Mix remaining ingredients; pour over chops. Cover and microwave 5 minutes. Let stand 5 minutes; turn and rearrange chops. Cover and microwave until tender, 5 to 8 minutes.

2 or 3 servings.

MINTED LAMB MEATBALLS

- 1 pound ground lamb
- 1 egg
- ¼ cup dry bread crumbs
- ¼ cup milk
- 2 tablespoons finely chopped onion
- ½ teaspoon salt
- ¼ teaspoon paprika
- ⅛ teaspoon pepper
- ¼ cup mint-flavored apple jelly
- ¼ teaspoon dried tarragon leaves

Mix all ingredients except jelly and tarragon. Shape into 12 meatballs, about 1¾ inches in diameter. Place in oblong baking dish, 10 x 6 x 1½ inches. Cover loosely and microwave on high (100%) 5 minutes; rearrange meatballs. Cover loosely and microwave until done, 1 to 2 minutes; drain.

Mix jelly and tarragon; spoon over meatballs. Cover loosely and microwave until jelly is melted, 1 to 2 minutes. Stir to coat meatballs evenly.

4 or 5 servings.

ORANGE-GLAZED CHICKEN

2½ - pound broiler-fryer chicken, cut up
 ½ cup orange marmalade
 ¼ cup orange juice
 2 tablespoons cornstarch
 2 tablespoons packed brown sugar
 2 tablespoons lemon juice
1½ teaspoons salt
 ½ orange, sliced and quartered

Arrange chicken pieces skin sides up and thickest parts to outside in oblong baking dish, 12 x 7½ x 2 inches. Cover loosely and microwave on high (100%) 15 minutes.

Mix marmalade, orange juice, cornstarch, brown sugar, lemon juice and salt in 4-cup glass measure. Spoon in juices from chicken. Microwave uncovered on high (100%) 2½ minutes; stir. Microwave to boiling, 1 to 1½ minutes. Boil until sauce is thickened and translucent, 1 minute longer. Stir in orange slices.

Spoon sauce over chicken. Cover loosely and microwave on high (100%) until chicken is done, 10 to 15 minutes. If desired, garnish with parsley.

6 servings.

MICROWAVE TIP

To ensure even cooking in the microwave, arrange chicken in the baking dish with the larger, meatier portions and pieces toward the edge of the dish and the smaller, less meaty pieces toward the center of the dish.

Pictured at left: Sunday dinner special — Orange-glazed Chicken (above), Buttered Broccoli (page 50) and Corn Muffins (page 62)

GOLDEN PARSLEYED CHICKEN

2½ - pound broiler-fryer chicken
 1 egg
 1 tablespoon water
30 round buttery crackers, finely crushed
       (about 1⅓ cups)
 2 tablespoons dried parsley flakes
 ½ teaspoon salt
 ⅛ teaspoon pepper

Cut chicken into pieces; cut each breast half into halves. Beat egg and water. Mix cracker crumbs, parsley, salt and pepper. Dip chicken pieces into egg mixture, then coat with crumbs. Arrange chicken skin sides up and thickest parts to outside in oblong baking dish, 12 x 7½ x 2 inches. Cover loosely and microwave on high (100%) until done, 20 to 25 minutes.

8 servings.

CHICKEN WITH TOMATOES AND RICE

 3 - pound broiler-fryer chicken
 1 can (8 ounces) stewed tomatoes
 1 can (8 ounces) tomato sauce
 2 medium onions, chopped
 1 medium green pepper, chopped
 1 clove garlic, finely chopped
 1 teaspoon salt
 ½ teaspoon ground thyme
 ½ teaspoon red pepper sauce
 ¼ teaspoon ground red pepper
 1 package (10 ounces) frozen whole okra
3½ cups hot cooked rice

Cut chicken into pieces; cut each breast half into halves. Mix all ingredients except okra and rice in 3-quart casserole. Cover and microwave on high (100%) 20 minutes. Stir in okra. Cover and microwave until chicken is done and okra is tender, 10 to 15 minutes. Serve over rice in bowls.

8 servings.

BARBECUED CHICKEN

2½ - pound broiler-fryer chicken
  1 cup catsup
  ½ cup water
  ¼ cup Worcestershire sauce
  ¼ cup vinegar
  ¼ cup packed brown sugar
  1 medium onion, chopped
  2 tablespoons cornstarch
  1 tablespoon lemon juice
  1 teaspoon salt
  1 teaspoon celery seed
  ¼ teaspoon liquid smoke
  2 dashes red pepper sauce

Cut chicken into pieces; cut each breast half into halves. Arrange chicken skin sides up and thickest parts to outside in oblong baking dish, 12 x 7½ x 2 inches. Mix remaining ingredients in 4-cup glass measure. Microwave uncovered on high (100%) 3 minutes; stir. Microwave until mixture boils and thickens, 2 to 3 minutes. Pour sauce over chicken.

Cover loosely and microwave on high (100%) 10 minutes. Rearrange chicken and baste with sauce. Cover loosely and microwave until chicken is done, 10 to 15 minutes, basting with sauce every 5 minutes.

8 servings.

CHICKEN WITH SAUCE SUPREME

2½ - pound broiler-fryer chicken
  1 teaspoon salt
  ⅛ teaspoon pepper
  1 can (10¾ ounces) condensed cream of
       chicken soup
  2 teaspoons dried parsley flakes
  1 can (16 ounces) whole onions, drained
  3 cups hot cooked rice

Cut chicken into pieces; cut each breast half into halves. Arrange chicken skin sides up and thickest parts to outside in oblong baking dish, 12 x 7½ x 2 inches. Sprinkle with salt and pepper.

Cover loosely and microwave on high (100%) until chicken is done, 20 to 25 minutes.

Remove chicken from dish; reserve juices. Stir soup and parsley into chicken juices. Arrange chicken in dish, coating with soup mixture. Add onions. Cover loosely and microwave until hot, 7 to 9 minutes. Serve with rice.

8 servings.

CHICKEN BREASTS WITH RICE

  1 jar (2½ ounces) dried beef
  2 medium stalks celery, chopped
  1 small onion, chopped
  1 tablespoon margarine or butter
  2 cups cooked rice
  2 tablespoons chopped parsley
  1 jar (1 ounce) pine nuts (optional)
  4 small chicken breast halves
       (about 1½ pounds)
  ½ teaspoon seasoned salt
       Paprika

Snip beef into small pieces. Cover and microwave beef, celery, onion and margarine in 2-quart casserole on high (100%) until onion is crisp-tender, 3 to 4 minutes. Stir in rice, parsley and pine nuts.

Arrange chicken breasts skin sides up and thickest parts to outside on rice mixture. Sprinkle with seasoned salt and paprika. Cover and microwave 5 minutes; turn casserole one-half turn. Microwave until chicken is done, 8 to 11 minutes.

4 servings.

CHICKEN, TETRAZZINI STYLE

- 4 chicken breast halves (about 2 pounds)
- ¼ cup margarine or butter
- 1 medium onion, chopped
- 1 small green pepper, chopped
- ¼ cup all-purpose flour
- 2 teaspoons instant chicken bouillon
- 1 teaspoon salt
- ⅛ teaspoon pepper
  Half-and-half
- ¼ cup dry white wine
- 1 jar (2 ounces) diced pimiento, drained
- 8 ounces fresh mushrooms, sliced
- 1 package (7 ounces) spaghetti, cooked and drained
- ¼ cup grated Parmesan cheese
- ½ cup sliced almonds

Arrange chicken breasts skin sides up and thickest parts to outside in 10-inch pie plate. Cover tightly and microwave on high (100%) 5 minutes; turn pie plate one-half turn. Microwave until chicken is done, 3 to 5 minutes. Let stand 5 minutes. Refrigerate until cool enough to handle, about 20 minutes. Remove meat from bones and skin; cut chicken into small pieces. Reserve chicken broth.

Cover loosely and microwave margarine, onion and green pepper in 2-quart casserole on high (100%) 2 minutes. Stir in flour, bouillon, salt and pepper. Add enough half-and-half to reserved chicken broth to measure 2 cups; stir into onion mixture. Stir in wine. Cover and microwave on medium-high (70%) until mixture boils and thickens, 8 to 10 minutes, stirring every 2 minutes. Stir in chicken, pimiento and mushrooms.

Place half of the spaghetti in 3-quart casserole; spread half of the chicken mixture over spaghetti. Repeat with remaining spaghetti and chicken mixture. Sprinkle with cheese; top with almonds. Cover and microwave on medium-high (70%) until hot, 15 to 18 minutes.

8 to 10 servings.

CURRIED CHICKEN BREASTS

- 1 medium onion, sliced and separated into rings
- ¼ cup margarine or butter
- 3 small chicken breasts (about 2 pounds), boned, skinned and halved
- ¼ cup half-and-half
- 2 teaspoons curry powder
- ½ teaspoon salt
- ¼ teaspoon ground ginger
- ⅛ teaspoon ground cumin
- 4 cups hot cooked rice
- ¼ cup dairy sour cream
  Accompaniments (chopped peanuts, toasted coconut, chutney, crisp bacon pieces, chopped tomatoes)

Cover loosely and microwave onion and margarine in oblong baking dish, 12 x 7½ x 2 inches, on high (100%) until margarine is melted, about 2 minutes. Place chicken breasts in dish, turning to coat with margarine. Arrange with thickest parts to the outside. Cover loosely and microwave 5 minutes; turn dish one-half turn.

Mix half-and-half, curry powder, salt, ginger and cumin; pour over chicken. Cover and microwave on medium-high (70%) until chicken is done, 3 to 5 minutes.

Remove chicken and place on rice on large platter. Mix sour cream into sauce until smooth. Spoon over chicken and rice. Serve with Accompaniments.

6 servings.

CORNISH HENS WITH BRUSSELS SPROUTS

1 package (8 ounces) frozen Brussels sprouts
1 medium onion, chopped
1 teaspoon salt
⅛ teaspoon pepper
1 cup shredded Swiss cheese (about 4 ounces)
3 frozen Rock Cornish hens (about 1¼ pounds each), thawed
¼ cup margarine or butter, melted
¾ teaspoon ground sage
½ teaspoon paprika
½ teaspoon bottled brown bouquet sauce

Cover and microwave Brussels sprouts, onion, salt and pepper in 1-quart casserole on high (100%) 5 minutes. Let stand until cool enough to handle, about 5 minutes. Cut each Brussels sprout into fourths; stir in cheese.

Remove giblets from hens. Stuff each hen with about ⅓ of the Brussels sprouts mixture. Secure opening with wooden skewer. Tie drumsticks together. Place hens breast sides down on microwave roasting rack in oblong baking dish, 12 x 7½ x 2 inches. Mix remaining ingredients; brush half of the mixture over hens.

Cover loosely and microwave on high (100%) 15 minutes. Turn hens breast sides up and rearrange; brush with remaining margarine mixture. Cover and microwave until done, 18 to 22 minutes. To serve, cut hens through stuffing with kitchen scissors, cutting through the breast and along backbone from tail to neck. Garnish with celery leaves and cherry tomatoes if desired.

6 servings.

TURKEY AND WILD RICE CASSEROLE

1 can (4 ounces) mushroom stems and pieces
3 tablespoons flour
1⅓ cups water
1½ teaspoons instant beef bouillon
½ teaspoon salt
1 package (6 ounces) long-grain and wild rice mix
2 packages (10 ounces each) frozen broccoli spears
2 cups cut-up cooked turkey

Mix mushrooms (with liquid) and flour in 4-cup glass measure. Stir in water, bouillon and salt. Microwave uncovered on high (100%) 3 minutes; stir. Microwave until mixture boils and thickens, 2 to 3 minutes, stirring every minute.

Pour rice (with seasoning mix) into oblong baking dish, 12 x 7½ x 2 inches. Add water and butter as directed on package. Cover and microwave on high (100%) 10 minutes. Let stand 5 minutes; stir. Cover and microwave until rice is tender, 7 to 9 minutes.

Microwave frozen broccoli in packages on high (100%) until tender, 10 to 12 minutes; drain.

Top rice with broccoli, turkey and mushroom sauce. Cover loosely and microwave on high (100%) until hot, 6 to 8 minutes.

6 servings.

FISH FILLETS WITH GARDEN VEGETABLES

Almond Crumb Topping (below)
1 pound fish fillets
5 green onions, sliced
2 medium zucchini, cut into ¼-inch slices
8 ounces fresh mushrooms, sliced
3 tablespoons margarine or butter, melted
1 teaspoon lemon juice
½ teaspoon salt
½ teaspoon dried oregano leaves
⅛ teaspoon pepper
2 medium tomatoes, each cut into
    6 wedges

Prepare Almond Crumb Topping. Arrange fish with thickest parts to outside in oval baking dish, 11½ x 7½ x 2 inches. Top with onions, zucchini and mushrooms. Mix margarine, lemon juice, salt, oregano and pepper; pour over fish and vegetables.

Cover tightly and microwave on high (100%) 5 minutes; turn dish one-half turn. Microwave until fish flakes easily with fork (175° on meat thermometer) and vegetables are crisp-tender, 6 to 8 minutes. Add tomatoes. Cover and microwave until tomatoes are hot, 1 to 2 minutes. Sprinkle with Almond Crumb Topping.

6 servings.

ALMOND CRUMB TOPPING
½ cup slivered almonds
1 teaspoon margarine or butter
1 cup buttermilk baking mix
3 tablespoons boiling water
2 tablespoons margarine or butter, softened
⅛ teaspoon garlic powder

Microwave almonds and 1 teaspoon margarine uncovered in 9-inch pie plate on high (100%) until light brown, 5 to 8 minutes, stirring every minute. Stir in remaining ingredients thoroughly with fork; spread evenly. Microwave 2 minutes; break up with fork and stir. Microwave until puffed and dry, 2 to 3 minutes. Break up with fork into about ¼-inch pieces.

Sensational fish story: Fish Fillets with Garden Vegetables

DILLED FISH

 2 tablespoons margarine or butter
½ pound fish fillets
¼ teaspoon dill weed
    Salt
    Pepper
    Lemon slices

Microwave margarine uncovered in square baking dish, 8 x 8 x 2 inches, on high (100%) until melted, 30 seconds to 1 minute. Place fillets in dish, turning to coat with margarine. Sprinkle with dill weed, salt and pepper. Cover tightly and microwave until fish flakes easily with fork (175° on meat thermometer) 2 to 2½ minutes. Garnish with lemon slices.

2 or 3 servings.

POACHED FISH

 1 pound fish fillets
 2 teaspoons instant chicken bouillon
½ cup water
¼ teaspoon salt
¼ teaspoon dried parsley flakes
¼ teaspoon chopped chives
 1 tablespoon lemon juice
 4 peppercorns
 1 small bay leaf
 6 lemon slices

If fillets are large, cut into serving pieces. Place in square baking dish, 8 x 8 x 2 inches. Sprinkle with instant bouillon.

Mix water, salt, parsley, chives, lemon juice, peppercorns and bay leaf; pour over fish. Top with lemon slices. Cover tightly and microwave on high (100%) until fish flakes easily with fork (175° on meat thermometer), 4½ to 5 minutes. Remove fish from broth with slotted spoon.

5 or 6 servings.

FISH-VEGETABLE MEDLEY

 1 pound fish fillets
 1 teaspoon salt
¼ teaspoon pepper
 1 package (10 ounces) frozen peas
 1 medium cucumber, cut lengthwise into fourths, then crosswise into 1-inch pieces
 1 medium stalk celery, cut diagonally into ¼-inch slices
 1 small onion, cut into ¼-inch slices
½ teaspoon salt
 1 tablespoon lemon juice
¼ cup margarine or butter

If fillets are large, cut into serving pieces. Place in 2-quart casserole. Sprinkle with 1 teaspoon salt and the pepper. Cover and microwave on high (100%) until fish is almost done, 3½ to 4 minutes.

Rinse frozen peas under running cold water to separate; drain. Spoon peas, cucumber, celery and onion onto fish; sprinkle with ½ teaspoon salt and the lemon juice. Dot with margarine. Cover and microwave until vegetables are crisp-tender and fish flakes easily with fork (175° on meat thermometer), about 6 minutes. Sprinkle with paprika and garnish with lemon wedges if desired.

5 or 6 servings.

TARTAR-SAUCED FILLETS

1   tablespoon margarine or butter
1   tablespoon flour
1   teaspoon instant chicken bouillon
⅛   teaspoon salt
½   cup water
¼   cup mayonnaise or salad dressing
1   tablespoon sweet pickle relish
1   teaspoon finely chopped onion
1   teaspoon lemon juice
1   package (14 ounces) frozen fried
      fish fillets

Microwave margarine uncovered in 2-cup glass measure on high (100%) until melted, 30 seconds to 1 minute. Stir in flour, bouillon, salt and water. Microwave 1 minute; stir. Microwave until sauce boils and thickens, 30 seconds to 1 minute. Stir in mayonnaise, relish, onion and lemon juice.

Arrange fillets in square baking dish, 8 x 8 x 2 inches. Cover loosely and microwave on high (100%) 5 minutes; turn dish one-quarter turn. Microwave until fish is hot (175° on meat thermometer), 3 to 4 minutes. Spoon sauce onto fish. Microwave uncovered until hot, 1 to 2 minutes.

4 servings.

TOMATO AND CHEESE FILLETS

1   tablespoon margarine or butter
½   pound fish fillets
¼   teaspoon salt
      Dash of pepper
2   teaspoons finely chopped onion
1   medium tomato, chopped
¼   cup shredded Cheddar cheese (about
      1 ounce)

Microwave margarine uncovered in square baking dish, 8 x 8 x 2 inches, on high (100%) until melted, 30 seconds to 1 minute. Place fish fillets in dish, turning to coat with margarine. Sprinkle with salt and pepper; top with onion, tomato and cheese. Cover tightly and microwave until fish flakes easily with fork (175° on meat thermometer) 2½ to 3 minutes.

2 or 3 servings.

SPANISH-STYLE HALIBUT

1   pound halibut, about 1 inch thick
½   teaspoon salt
2   tablespoons olive or vegetable oil
½   cup thinly sliced green onions
½   cup chopped green pepper
1   clove garlic, finely chopped
1   can (8 ounces) whole tomatoes, drained
      and chopped
1   tablespoon lemon juice
¼   teaspoon red pepper sauce

Cut fish into serving pieces. Place fish in oblong baking dish, 12 x 7½ x 2 inches. Sprinkle with salt.

Mix oil, onions, green pepper and garlic in 1-quart casserole. Cover tightly and microwave on high (100%) 1 minute; stir. Cover and microwave until green pepper is crisp-tender, 1 to 2 minutes. Mix in remaining ingredients; spoon over fish.

Cover tightly and microwave on high (100%) 4 minutes; turn dish one-quarter turn. Microwave until fish flakes easily with fork (175° on meat thermometer), 4 to 6 minutes.

4 servings.

STUFFED SOLE RINGS

 1 package (10 ounces) frozen chopped
      broccoli
¼ cup mayonnaise or salad dressing
¼ cup chopped almonds or pecans
 1 tablespoon lemon juice
¼ teaspoon salt
 1 pound sole fillets
¼ teaspoon salt
⅛ teaspoon pepper

Microwave frozen broccoli in package on high (100%) until thawed, 4 to 5 minutes; drain. Mix with mayonnaise, almonds, lemon juice and ¼ teaspoon salt.

Sprinkle fillets with ¼ teaspoon salt and the pepper. Cut fillets lengthwise into strips, 1½ to 2 inches wide. Bring ends of each strip together, forming a circle about 2 inches in diameter; fasten ends with wooden pick. Arrange in square baking dish, 8 x 8 x 2 inches. Spoon broccoli mixture into center of each circle. Cover tightly and microwave on high (100%) until fish flakes easily with fork (175° on meat thermometer), 5 to 6½ minutes.

5 or 6 servings.

COD, CONTINENTAL STYLE

 6 to 8 large romaine leaves
 1 - pound cod fillet, about 1 inch thick
½ teaspoon salt
 2 cloves garlic, crushed
 2 green onions
¼ cup thinly sliced radishes
 2 tablespoons lemon juice
 1 tablespoon olive or vegetable oil
      Lemon wedges

Pour boiling water over romaine leaves. Let stand until limp, about 2 minutes; drain. Arrange half of the leaves on microwave roasting rack in oblong baking dish, 12 x 7½ x 2 inches. Place fish on leaves. Rub salt and garlic over fish. Arrange onions and radishes on fish; pour lemon juice and oil over fish. Place remaining leaves on top of fish.

Cover loosely and microwave on high (100%) 5 minutes; turn dish one-half turn. Microwave until fish flakes easily with fork (175° on meat thermometer), 8 to 10 minutes, turning dish one-half turn every 4 minutes. Remove leaves. Serve fish with lemon wedges.

4 servings.

CRUNCHY TUNA CASSEROLE

 1 can (16 ounces) cut green beans
 1 can (10¾ ounces) condensed cream of
      mushroom soup
 1 can (3 ounces) French fried onions
 2 cans (6½ ounces each) tuna, drained
 1 cup thinly sliced celery
 2 tablespoons chopped pimiento
 1 tablespoon soy sauce

Drain green beans, reserving ¼ cup liquid. Mix soup and reserved bean liquid. Fold half of the onions and the remaining ingredients into soup mixture. Pour into 2-quart casserole. Cover tightly and microwave on high (100%) until hot, 5 to 7 minutes; stir. Sprinkle with remaining onions. Microwave uncovered 2 minutes.

6 servings.

Pictured at right: An attractive and economical microwave menu — Stuffed Sole Rings (this page), Herbed Potatoes (page 55) and Cheese-crumbed Tomatoes (page 59)

TUNA SHELLS

1   jar (15½ ounces) spaghetti sauce
1   teaspoon Italian seasoning
1   teaspoon instant minced onion
1   egg
½   cup small curd cottage cheese
1   can (9¼ ounces) tuna, drained and
        flaked
1   cup shredded mozzarella cheese
        (about 4 ounces)
2   tablespoons grated Parmesan cheese
1   jar (2 ounces) diced pimiento, drained
1   tablespoon dried parsley flakes
15   uncooked jumbo macaroni shells
        (about 5 ounces), cooked, drained
        and cooled

Mix spaghetti sauce, Italian seasoning and instant onion; pour ½ cup into oblong baking
dish, 12 x 7½ x 2 inches. Beat egg; stir in cottage
cheese, tuna, mozzarella cheese, Parmesan
cheese, pimiento and parsley. Fill macaroni
shells with cheese mixture. Arrange filled shells
on sauce in dish. Spoon remaining sauce over
shells, covering shells completely.

Cover tightly and microwave on medium-high
(70%) 5 minutes; turn dish one-half turn. Microwave until hot, 5 to 8 minutes. Garnish with
chopped parsley if desired.

5 servings.

MICROWAVE TIPS

Canned fish such as tuna, salmon or
shrimp can be microwaved after mixing into casseroles, sandwich fillings
and salads. Microwave just long enough
to cook the ingredients combined with
the fish.

Fish fillets should be microwaved with
the thickest pieces to the outside of the
dish. Remember, overcooking causes
toughness.

SEAFOOD CREPES

1   package (10 ounces) frozen chopped
        spinach
⅓   cup margarine or butter
¼   cup all-purpose flour
1   can (13¾ ounces) chicken broth
        (1¾ cups)
½   teaspoon salt
        Dash of pepper
1   tablespoon lemon juice
1   can (6½ ounces) tuna, drained
1   can (4½ ounces) medium shrimp,
        drained
1   cup shredded Swiss cheese (about
        4 ounces)
12   crepes (8 to 10 inches in diameter)
        Dried parsley flakes

Microwave frozen spinach in package on high
(100%) until thawed, 4 to 5 minutes; drain.

Microwave margarine uncovered in 4-cup glass
measure on high (100%) until melted, 30 seconds to 1 minute. Stir in flour, broth, salt and
pepper. Microwave 2 minutes; stir. Microwave
until mixture boils and thickens, 1½ to 2 minutes, stirring every minute. Stir in lemon juice.

Mix spinach, tuna, shrimp, cheese and ¾ cup of
the sauce. Place slightly rounded ¼ cup sea-
food mixture in center of each crepe. Roll up
crepes; place seam sides down in row in oblong
baking dish, 12 x 7½ x 2 inches. Pour remaining
sauce over rolls; sprinkle with parsley. Cover
loosely and microwave on high (100%) until
hot, 6 to 7 minutes.

6 servings.

INDIVIDUAL SALMON LOAVES

1 can (16 ounces) salmon, drained and flaked
2 eggs, beaten
⅓ cup dry bread crumbs
2 tablespoons milk
½ teaspoon grated lemon peel
½ teaspoon chopped chives
½ teaspoon salt
Creamed Peas (below)

Mix all ingredients except Creamed Peas. Press into 6 six-ounce custard cups. Arrange cups in circle in microwave. Microwave uncovered on high (100%) 3 minutes; rearrange cups. Microwave until set, 1½ to 2½ minutes.

Prepare Creamed Peas. Invert salmon loaves on serving plate; serve with peas.

6 servings.

CREAMED PEAS

1 tablespoon margarine or butter
1 tablespoon flour
½ teaspoon salt
Dash of pepper
⅔ cup milk
1 package (10 ounces) frozen peas, cooked and drained

Microwave margarine uncovered in 2-cup glass measure on high (100%) until melted, 30 seconds to 1 minute. Blend in flour, salt and pepper; stir in milk. Microwave 1 minute. Stir in peas. Microwave until mixture boils and thickens, 1 to 2 minutes.

SALMON-RICE BAKE

1 package (10 ounces) frozen chopped broccoli, broken apart
1½ cups instant rice
1¼ cups water
1 can (10¾ ounces) condensed cream of mushroom soup
1 can (7¾ ounces) salmon, drained and flaked
2 tablespoons margarine or butter
½ teaspoon salt

Mix all ingredients in 1½-quart casserole. Cover and microwave on high (100%) 5 minutes; stir. Cover and microwave until rice is tender, 6 to 7 minutes. Stir before serving.

4 servings.

CRAB AND SHRIMP EN CASSEROLE

2 tablespoons margarine or butter
⅓ cup dry bread crumbs
1 medium green pepper, chopped
1 medium onion, chopped
2 medium stalks celery, chopped
1 can (6½ ounces) crabmeat, drained and cartilage removed
1 can (4½ ounces) shrimp, rinsed and drained
1 teaspoon Worcestershire sauce
½ teaspoon salt
⅛ teaspoon pepper
1 cup mayonnaise or salad dressing

Microwave margarine uncovered in custard cup on high (100%) until melted, 30 seconds to 1 minute. Mix in bread crumbs. Microwave until crisp and golden brown, about 2 minutes, stirring once or twice.

Microwave green pepper, onion and celery uncovered in 1-quart casserole on high (100%) until crisp-tender, 2 to 3 minutes. Stir in remaining ingredients. Microwave on medium-high (70%) until hot, 6 to 8 minutes. Sprinkle with bread crumbs.

6 servings.

EGGS IN TOAST CUPS

2 slices bread
2 tablespoons margarine or butter,
   softened
2 eggs
  Salt
  Pepper

Flatten bread slices with rolling pin to ¼-inch thickness. Spread one side of each slice with margarine. Press each slice buttered side down into 6-ounce custard cup. Microwave uncovered on high (100%) 1 minute; rearrange cups. Microwave until crisp, 1 to 1½ minutes.

Break an egg into each cup. Microwave uncovered until eggs are set, 1 to 1½ minutes. Sprinkle with salt and pepper.

2 servings.

MEXICAN-STYLE EGG CUPS

4 eggs
¼ cup milk
¼ teaspoon salt
  Dash of pepper
2 tablespoons chopped green chilies
4 flour tortillas (6 inches in diameter)
1 medium tomato, chopped
½ cup shredded Monterey Jack or Colby
   cheese (about 2 ounces)
  Taco sauce (optional)

Beat eggs, milk, salt and pepper in 1-quart casserole. Cover and microwave on high (100%) 2 minutes; stir. Cover and microwave until set but still moist, 1 to 1½ minutes. Stir in chilies, breaking up eggs.

Line 4 custard or coffee cups with tortillas. Divide egg mixture among cups; top with tomato and cheese. Microwave uncovered on high (100%) until cheese is melted, 1½ to 2½ minutes. Serve with taco sauce.

4 servings.

SCRAMBLED EGGS

4 eggs
¼ cup milk
¼ teaspoon salt
  Dash of pepper

Beat all ingredients with fork in 1-quart casserole. If desired, stir in ¼ cup shredded cheese, crumbled cooked bacon, chopped fully cooked ham, chopped chives or green onions or chopped canned mushrooms. Cover and microwave on high (100%) until eggs are puffy and set but still moist, 3 to 4 minutes, stirring every minute. Stir before serving.

2 servings.

Note: Recipe can be doubled. Increase microwave time to 6 to 8 minutes, stirring every 2 minutes.

MICROWAVE TIPS

Do not microwave eggs in their shells. Pressure will build up and the eggs will explode! However, eggs can be hardcooked conventionally, sliced and added to a microwaved cream or cheese sauce.

Whole shelled eggs can be poached or steamed in the microwave. Pierce the yolk with a wooden pick, cover tightly and microwave on medium (50%) until eggs are almost set. Eggs will continue to cook while standing.

SCRAMBLED EGGS BENEDICT

1 package (1¼ ounces) hollandaise sauce
    mix
4 to 8 thin slices Canadian-style bacon or
    smoked ham
4 eggs
¼ cup milk
2 tablespoons chopped green pepper
    (optional)
⅛ teaspoon salt
    Dash of pepper
2 English muffins, split and toasted

Mix sauce as directed on package in 2-cup glass measure. Microwave uncovered on high (100%) 1 minute; stir. Microwave until mixture boils and thickens, 1 to 1½ minutes, stirring every 30 seconds.

Cover and microwave bacon on high (100%) until hot, 1½ to 2 minutes.

Beat eggs in 1-quart casserole. Beat in milk, green pepper, salt and pepper. Cover and microwave on high (100%) 2 minutes; stir. Cover and microwave until eggs are set but still moist, 1 to 1½ minutes.

Place muffins cut sides up on serving plate. Top each with bacon slice and large spoonful of eggs; spoon sauce over eggs. Microwave uncovered on high (100%) until hot, 1 to 1½ minutes.

4 servings.

RED FLANNEL HASH WITH EGGS

2 slices bacon, cut into 1-inch pieces
1 medium onion, chopped
2 cans (15 ounces each) corned beef hash
1 can (8¼ ounces) sliced beets, drained
    and coarsely chopped
6 eggs
    Salt
    Pepper

Place bacon and onion in round baking dish, 9 x 2 inches. Cover loosely and microwave on high (100%) 2 minutes; stir. Cover and microwave until onion is tender, 2 to 3 minutes. Stir in hash; break up hash with fork. Stir in beets. Cover and microwave until mixture is hot, 4 to 5 minutes, stirring once.

Press back of spoon around edge of mixture to make 6 indentations. Break an egg into each indentation; pierce yolk with wooden pick. Cover tightly and microwave on medium-high (70%) until eggs are almost set, 5 to 6 minutes, turning dish one-quarter turn every 2 minutes. Let stand 3 minutes, depending on desired doneness. (Eggs will continue to cook while standing.) Season with salt and pepper.

6 servings.

EGGS FLORENTINE

- 2 packages (10 ounces each) frozen chopped spinach
- 2 tablespoons margarine or butter
- 2 tablespoons flour
- ½ teaspoon salt
- ½ teaspoon instant minced onion
- ¼ teaspoon dry mustard
  Dash of pepper
- 1 cup milk
- ⅓ cup shredded Cheddar cheese (about 1½ ounces)
- 1 tablespoon lemon juice
- 6 eggs
  Salt
  Pepper
- 1 tablespoon margarine or butter
- ¼ cup dry bread crumbs

Microwave frozen spinach in packages on high (100%) until thawed, 7 to 8 minutes; drain.

Microwave 2 tablespoons margarine uncovered in 2-cup glass measure on high (100%) until melted, 30 seconds to 1 minute. Blend in flour, salt, the onion, mustard and dash of pepper. Stir in milk. Microwave 1½ minutes; stir. Microwave until mixture boils and thickens, 2 to 2½ minutes, stirring every minute. Stir in cheese and lemon juice.

Mix spinach and half of the cheese sauce in oblong baking dish, 9½ x 7½ x 2 inches; spread evenly in dish. Make 6 indentations in spinach; break an egg into each. Sprinkle with salt and pepper. Pour remaining sauce around eggs. Cover loosely and microwave on high (100%) 6 minutes; turn dish one-quarter turn. Microwave until eggs are done, 3 to 4 minutes.

Microwave 1 tablespoon margarine uncovered in 1-cup glass measure on high (100%) until melted, 30 seconds to 1 minute. Stir in bread crumbs; sprinkle over eggs.

6 servings.

DEVILED EGGS AND NOODLES

- Deviled Eggs (below)
- 2 tablespoons chopped onion
- 1 tablespoon margarine or butter
- 2½ cups noodles, cooked
- 1 cup dairy sour cream
- ⅓ cup grated Parmesan cheese
- ⅓ cup milk
- ⅓ cup sliced ripe olives
- 2 teaspoons poppy seed
- ½ teaspoon salt

Prepare Deviled Eggs. Cover and microwave onion and margarine in 1½-quart casserole on high (100%) until onion is tender, 1½ to 2 minutes. Stir in remaining ingredients. Cover and microwave until hot, 5 to 6 minutes; stir.

Arrange eggs on noodles. Cover and microwave until eggs are hot, 1 to 2 minutes.

4 servings.

DEVILED EGGS
- 3 hard-cooked eggs
- 2 tablespoons mayonnaise or salad dressing
- ½ teaspoon prepared mustard
- ⅛ teaspoon salt
  Dash of pepper

Cut eggs lengthwise into halves. Slip out yolks; mash with fork. Mix in remaining ingredients. Fill whites with yolk mixture, heaping it up lightly.

◀Microwave the frozen spinach in the paper packages. Remove the printed waxed paper covering to avoid staining the microwave floor. Microwave until thawed, 7 to 8 minutes.

▶ Make 6 indentations in the spinach with the back of a spoon being careful not to expose the baking dish surface (the eggs might stick). Break an egg into each indentation.

For an elegant brunch: Eggs Florentine (page 42) and Oniony French Bread (page 62)

EGG FOO YONG CASSEROLE

Sauce (below)
¼ cup chopped onion
½ cup chopped celery
½ cup chopped green pepper
1 tablespoon margarine or butter
1 can (16 ounces) bean sprouts, drained
⅓ cup sliced water chestnuts
1 tablespoon chopped pimiento
¾ teaspoon salt
6 eggs, beaten

Prepare Sauce. Cover and microwave onion, celery, green pepper and margarine in 1½-quart casserole on high (100%) 2½ minutes; stir. Cover and microwave until vegetables are almost tender, 2 to 2½ minutes.

Stir in remaining ingredients. Cover and microwave until eggs are set but still moist, 5 to 6 minutes, stirring every 2 minutes. Spoon Sauce over each serving.

5 to 6 servings.

SAUCE

⅔ cup water
1 tablespoon cornstarch
1 tablespoon soy sauce
1 teaspoon sugar
1½ teaspoons vinegar

Mix all ingredients in 2-cup glass measure. Microwave uncovered on high (100%) 1 minute; stir. Microwave until mixture boils and thickens, 1 to 1½ minutes, stirring every minute.

CREAMED EGGS ON TOAST

3 tablespoons margarine or butter
3 tablespoons flour
½ teaspoon dry mustard
¼ teaspoon salt
Dash of pepper
1½ cups milk
4 hard-cooked eggs, each cut into eighths
1 teaspoon dried parsley flakes
4 slices buttered toast

Microwave margarine uncovered in 1-quart casserole on high (100%) until melted, 30 seconds to 1 minute. Blend in flour, mustard, salt and pepper. Stir in milk. Microwave 2 minutes; stir. Microwave until mixture boils and thickens, 2 to 3 minutes, stirring every minute. Gently stir in eggs and parsley. Serve over toast.

4 servings.

SPECIAL MACARONI AND CHEESE

4 slices bacon
2 cups macaroni, cooked
2 cups ½-inch cubes process American cheese (about 10 ounces)
¼ cup milk
¼ teaspoon salt
Dash of pepper

Place bacon in 1½-quart casserole. Cover loosely and microwave on high (100%) until crisp, 3 to 4 minutes. Remove bacon; reserve.

Pour off all but 1 tablespoon bacon drippings. Add remaining ingredients to drippings in casserole. Cover and microwave 3 minutes; stir. Cover and microwave until hot, 3 to 4 minutes. Crumble bacon and sprinkle over top.

4 to 6 servings.

DEVILED HAM QUICHE

9 - inch Cornmeal Pie Shell (page 46)
1   cup shredded mozzarella cheese (about
      4 ounces)
¼ cup finely chopped green onions
3   eggs
1   egg yolk
1   can (13 ounces) evaporated milk
½ teaspoon salt
¼ teaspoon red pepper sauce
1   can (4½ ounces) deviled ham

Prepare and microwave pie shell. Sprinkle cheese and onions in pie shell. Beat eggs, egg yolk, evaporated milk, salt and pepper sauce in 4-cup glass measure; stir in deviled ham. Microwave uncovered on medium-high (70%) until hot, 4 minutes, stirring every minute. Pour carefully into pie shell.

Microwave uncovered on inverted dinner plate on medium-high (70%) 5 minutes; turn dish one-half turn. Microwave until center is almost set, 5 to 8 minutes. Cover loosely and let stand 10 minutes. (Center will continue to cook while standing.)

6 servings.

MICROWAVE TIPS

Cheese can become rubbery and tough if overcooked. Microwave cheese at a lower power setting, medium-high (70%), or cook for a very short time on high (100%).

Shredded process cheese blends easily with other ingredients in sauces and soups. Grated hard cheese, such as Parmesan, is a flavorful addition to vegetables and makes a nice topping for microwaved casseroles.

CORN PUDDING QUICHE

9 - inch Cornmeal Pie Shell (right)
6 slices bacon
¼ cup finely chopped green onions
1 cup shredded Swiss cheese (about
     4 ounces)
4 eggs
2 tablespoons flour
1 can (5⅓ ounces) evaporated milk
1 cup milk
1 teaspoon salt
1 can (8½ ounces) cream-style corn
   Paprika

Prepare and microwave pie shell. Place bacon on microwave roasting rack in oblong baking dish, 12 x 7½ x 2 inches. Cover loosely and microwave on high (100%) until crisp, 3 to 4 minutes; cool bacon and crumble. Sprinkle bacon, onions and cheese in pie shell.

Beat eggs, flour, evaporated milk, milk and salt in 4-cup glass measure; stir in corn. Microwave uncovered on medium-high (70%) until warm and slightly thickened, 5 to 7 minutes, stirring every 2 minutes. Pour carefully into pie shell.

Microwave uncovered on inverted dinner plate on medium-high (70%) until center is almost set, 11 to 14 minutes, turning dish one-quarter turn every 3 minutes. Sprinkle with paprika. Cover loosely and let stand 15 minutes. (Center will continue to cook while standing.)

6 servings.

VEGETABLES AND BREADS

ASPARAGUS-ALMOND SAUTE

¼ cup sliced or slivered almonds
2 tablespoons margarine or butter
3 cups 1-inch pieces asparagus (about
    1¼ pounds)*
1 cup sliced mushrooms*
1 small clove garlic, minced
½ teaspoon seasoned salt

Combine almonds and margarine in 1-quart casserole. Microwave uncovered on high (100%) until almonds are toasted, 4 to 5 minutes, stirring every minute. Remove almonds with slotted spoon; reserve.

Add asparagus, mushrooms and garlic to drippings in casserole. Cover and microwave until asparagus is tender, 8 to 9 minutes. Stir in salt; sprinkle with reserved almonds.

4 or 5 servings.

*1 package (10 ounces) frozen asparagus, broken apart, and 1 can (4 ounces) mushroom stems and pieces, drained, can be substituted for the fresh asparagus and mushrooms.

SWEET-AND-SOUR BEANS

2 slices bacon
1 small onion, sliced
¼ cup sugar
1 tablespoon flour
    Dash of pepper
⅓ cup vinegar
1 can (16 ounces) cut green beans,
    drained
1 can (16 ounces) wax beans, drained

Place bacon in 1½-quart casserole. Cover loosely and microwave on high (100%) until crisp, 2 to 3 minutes. Remove bacon and drain.

Add onion to bacon fat in casserole. Cover and microwave until onion is crisp-tender, 2 to 3 minutes.

Stir in sugar, flour, pepper and vinegar. Cover and microwave to boiling, 1½ to 2 minutes.

Stir in beans. Cover and microwave until hot, 3 to 3½ minutes. Crumble bacon; sprinkle over top.

5 servings.

GREEN BEANS AND BAMBOO SHOOTS

1 package (10 ounces) frozen French-style
   green beans
⅓ cup bamboo shoots, cut into ½-inch
   pieces
1 tablespoon margarine or butter
¼ teaspoon salt
¼ teaspoon sugar
¼ teaspoon ground ginger

Cover and microwave frozen green beans in 1-quart casserole on high (100%) until tender, 6 to 7 minutes; drain.

Stir in remaining ingredients. Microwave uncovered until hot, about 1 minute.

4 or 5 servings.

BEAN AND ONION BAKE

1 package (10 ounces) frozen French-style
   green beans
1 package (9 ounces) frozen onions in
   cheese sauce
½ to 1 can (8½ ounce) water chestnuts,
   drained and sliced
¼ teaspoon salt

Microwave frozen green beans in package on high (100%) until tender, 8 to 9 minutes; drain.

Cut small slit in onion pouch; microwave onions on high (100%) until hot, 6 to 7 minutes.

Mix green beans, onions, water chestnuts and salt in 1½-quart casserole. Cover and microwave on high (100%) until hot, 2 to 3 minutes.

5 servings.

Pictured at left: Offer a garden-fresh choice. Clockwise from top — Cauliflower with Cheese Sauce (page 52), Red Cabbage and Ham (page 51) and Italian-style Cucumbers (page 54)

VEGETABLE MEDLEY

1 package (6 ounces) hash brown
   potatoes with onions
1 can (11 ounces) condensed Cheddar
   cheese soup
1 can (16 ounces) French-style green
   beans, drained
1 can (2.8 ounces) French fried onions
¼ teaspoon salt
⅛ teaspoon pepper
⅛ teaspoon dry mustard

Pour enough boiling water over potatoes to cover in 2-quart casserole or bowl. Let stand 5 minutes; drain thoroughly.

Reserve ½ cup of the onions; stir remaining onions and remaining ingredients into potatoes. Cover and microwave on high (100%) 5 minutes; stir. Top with reserved onions. Cover and microwave until hot and bubbly, 4 to 5 minutes.

8 servings.

SAVORY LIMAS WITH PEAS

1 package (10 ounces) frozen lima beans
¼ cup water
1 package (10 ounces) frozen peas
½ teaspoon salt
¼ teaspoon dried savory leaves
¼ teaspoon dry mustard
2 tablespoons margarine or butter

Cover and microwave frozen lima beans and water in 1½-quart casserole on high (100%) 3 minutes; drain.

Stir in remaining ingredients. Cover and microwave until vegetables are tender, 5 to 7 minutes. Let stand 5 minutes.

3 or 4 servings.

BROCCOLI WITH HOLLANDAISE

1 pound broccoli
¼ cup water
½ teaspoon salt
   Hollandaise Sauce (below)

Cut broccoli lengthwise into thin stalks. If stems are thicker than 1 inch, make lengthwise gashes in each stem. Place water and salt in oblong baking dish, 12 x 7½ x 2 inches. Arrange broccoli with tips in center of dish. Cover tightly and microwave on high (100%) 3 minutes; turn dish one-half turn. Microwave until tender, 3 to 5 minutes; drain. Prepare Hollandaise Sauce; pour over broccoli.

6 servings.

HOLLANDAISE SAUCE
6 tablespoons margarine or butter
2 tablespoons lemon juice
1 tablespoon water
2 egg yolks

Microwave margarine uncovered in 2-cup glass measure on high (100%) until just melted, 30 to 45 seconds. Stir in lemon juice and water. Beat in egg yolks with fork. Microwave on medium (50%) until slightly thickened, 45 seconds to 1½ minutes, stirring every 15 seconds. (Do not overcook or sauce will curdle.) Let stand 1 minute. (Sauce will thicken while standing.)

BROCCOLI ITALIANO

1 pound broccoli
2 tablespoons water
2 tablespoons vegetable oil
1 clove garlic, minced
1 tablespoon vinegar
½ teaspoon salt
¼ teaspoon Italian seasoning
1 tablespoon margarine or butter
2 tablespoons dry bread crumbs
2 tablespoons grated Parmesan cheese

Arrange broccoli with tips in center of dish. Add water. Cover and microwave on high (100%) until broccoli is tender, 8 to 10 minutes; drain. Mix oil, garlic, vinegar, salt and Italian seasoning; pour over broccoli.

Microwave margarine uncovered in small dish on high (100%) until melted, 30 seconds to 1 minute. Stir in bread crumbs and cheese. Sprinkle over broccoli. Microwave uncovered on high (100%) until hot, 1 to 2 minutes.

5 or 6 servings.

BUTTERED BROCCOLI

2 packages (10 ounces each) frozen
   broccoli spears
1 clove garlic, minced
¼ teaspoon dried rosemary leaves
¼ teaspoon salt
2 tablespoons margarine or butter
¼ cup crushed salad croutons (optional)

Microwave frozen broccoli in packages on high (100%) until almost tender, 10 to 12 minutes; drain. Place broccoli in 1½-quart casserole or serving dish.

Sprinkle broccoli with garlic, rosemary and salt; dot with margarine. Cover and microwave on high (100%) until margarine melts, 1 to 2 minutes. Toss lightly; sprinkle with croutons.

5 or 6 servings.

BROCCOLI, CHEESE AND TOMATO BAKE

2 packages (10 ounces each) frozen
    broccoli spears
1 package (1.25 ounces) cheese sauce mix
2 medium tomatoes, sliced
½ cup croutons, crushed

Microwave frozen broccoli in packages on high (100%) until almost tender, 10 to 12 minutes; drain. Place broccoli in 1½-quart serving dish.

Prepare cheese sauce mix as directed on package in 2-cup glass measure. Microwave uncovered on high (100%) 1½ minutes; stir. Microwave to boiling, 1½ to 2 minutes.

Arrange tomato slices on broccoli. Top with cheese sauce; sprinkle with croutons. Microwave uncovered on high (100%) until hot, 2 to 3 minutes.

8 servings.

BUTTERED CABBAGE WEDGES

½ medium head cabbage, cut into 4 to 6
    wedges
2 tablespoons water
½ teaspoon caraway seed
2 tablespoons margarine or butter
    Salt

Arrange cabbage wedges with narrow ends toward center in dish. Add water; sprinkle with caraway seed. Cover and microwave on high (100%) 7 minutes; turn dish one-quarter turn. Microwave until crisp-tender, 5 to 6 minutes; drain.

Microwave margarine uncovered in small dish until melted, 30 seconds to 1 minute; drizzle over cabbage. Sprinkle with salt.

4 to 6 servings.

RED CABBAGE AND HAM

5 cups finely shredded red cabbage (about
    1¼ pounds)
¼ cup apple juice
2 tablespoons vegetable oil
½ cup chopped celery
1 medium onion, chopped
1 teaspoon salt
½ teaspoon dried rosemary leaves,
    crushed
⅛ teaspoon pepper
2 cloves garlic, finely chopped
1 cup diced fully cooked smoked ham
2 tablespoons red wine vinegar

Mix cabbage, apple juice, oil, celery, onion, salt, rosemary, pepper and garlic in 3-quart casserole. Cover and microwave on high (100%) 5 minutes; stir. Cover and microwave until cabbage is crisp-tender, 5 to 8 minutes.

Stir in ham and vinegar. Cover and microwave until ham is hot, 2 to 4 minutes.

6 to 8 servings.

SWEET-AND-SOUR CARROTS

2 cups ¼-inch diagonally sliced carrots
¼ cup bottled French dressing
1 teaspoon sugar
½ teaspoon salt
1 tablespoon soy sauce
1 small green pepper, cut into ¼-inch strips
¼ cup chopped green onions

Mix carrots, French dressing, sugar, salt and soy sauce in 1½-quart casserole. Cover and microwave on high (100%) 6 minutes.

Stir in green pepper and onions. Microwave until carrots are crisp-tender, 5 to 7 minutes.

4 servings.

ORANGE-BUTTERED CARROTS

4 cups sliced carrots
3 tablespoons margarine or butter
1 tablespoon sugar
2 teaspoons grated orange peel
½ teaspoon salt

Cover and microwave carrots in 1-quart casserole or bowl on high (100%) 5 minutes. Let stand 5 minutes; stir. Cover and microwave until carrots are tender, 5 to 6 minutes; drain. Stir in remaining ingredients.

5 or 6 servings.

CAULIFLOWER WITH CHEESE SAUCE

1 medium head cauliflower (about
  1½ pounds)
2 tablespoons water
1 jar (8 ounces) pasteurized process
  cheese spread
1 tomato, chopped (optional)

Cut and remove a cone-shaped piece from center of cauliflower core. Place cauliflower core end down in dish; add water. Cover and microwave on high (100%) until cauliflower is just tender, 8 to 10 minutes; drain.

Remove cover from cheese spread; microwave cheese spread (in jar) on high (100%) until softened, 30 seconds to 1 minute. Pour over cauliflower. Garnish with tomato.

6 servings.

BUTTERED CORN ON THE COB

¼ cup margarine or butter
1 tablespoon chopped chives
1 package (4 ears) frozen corn on the cob
  Grated Parmesan cheese (optional)

Microwave margarine and chives uncovered in baking dish on high (100%) until margarine is melted, 30 seconds to 1 minute.

Arrange corn in baking dish, turning to coat with margarine. Cover loosely and microwave 6 minutes; turn and rearrange ears. Cover loosely and microwave until corn is done, 3 to 5 minutes. Sprinkle with cheese.

4 servings.

CREAMED CORN

3 slices bacon
2 tablespoons chopped onion
1 tablespoon chopped green pepper
1 tablespoon flour
½ cup dairy sour cream
1 can (16 ounces) whole kernel corn,
  drained

Place bacon in 1-quart casserole. Cover loosely and microwave on high (100%) until crisp, 2½ to 3 minutes. Remove bacon and drain.

Add onion and green pepper to bacon fat in casserole. Cover and microwave until vegetables are tender, 2½ to 3 minutes.

Stir in flour, sour cream and corn. Cover and microwave 2 minutes; stir. Cover and microwave until hot, 1 to 2 minutes. Crumble bacon; sprinkle over corn.

5 servings.

Pictured at right: A sure-to-be-remembered menu — Individual Salmon Loaves (page 39), Orange-buttered Carrots (this page) and Cheesy Hash Browns (page 56)

ITALIAN-STYLE CUCUMBERS

2 medium cucumbers, each cut lengthwise into fourths then crosswise into ½-inch pieces
1 large onion, sliced and separated into rings
2 tablespoons firm margarine or butter, cut into small pieces
1 teaspoon salt
½ teaspoon Italian seasoning
⅛ teaspoon pepper
2 cloves garlic, finely chopped

Mix all ingredients in 2-quart casserole. Cover and microwave on high (100%) 3 minutes; stir. Cover and microwave until vegetables are crisp-tender, 4 to 5 minutes.

8 servings.

RATATOUILLE

1 small eggplant (about 1 pound), cut into ½-inch cubes
1 medium onion, sliced
2 cloves garlic, finely chopped
2 tablespoons olive or vegetable oil
1 teaspoon salt
½ teaspoon dried basil leaves
¼ teaspoon pepper
1 medium green pepper, cut into ¼-inch strips
2 medium zucchini, cut into ¼-inch slices
3 medium tomatoes, each cut into eighths
¼ cup chopped parsley

Mix eggplant, onion, garlic and oil in 3-quart casserole. Cover and microwave on high (100%) 4 minutes.

Stir in salt, basil, pepper, green pepper and zucchini. Cover and microwave 6 minutes.

Stir in tomatoes and parsley. Microwave uncovered until vegetables are crisp-tender, 1 to 2 minutes.

8 servings.

GARLIC MUSHROOMS

12 ounces large fresh mushrooms (about 12)
¼ cup finely chopped green onions
3 cloves garlic, finely chopped
3 tablespoons margarine or butter
½ cup soft bread crumbs
¼ teaspoon salt
¼ teaspoon ground thyme
⅛ teaspoon pepper

Cut stems from mushrooms; chop finely. Mix chopped stems, onions, garlic and margarine in 1-quart casserole. Microwave uncovered on high (100%) until onions are crisp-tender, 2 to 3 minutes, stirring once. Stir in remaining ingredients.

Fill mushroom caps with stuffing mixture. Arrange mushrooms filled sides up and smallest mushrooms in center in 10-inch pie plate. Cover loosely and microwave 2 minutes; turn pie plate one-half turn. Microwave until hot, 1 to 2 minutes.

6 servings.

MICROWAVE TIPS

You will find that vegetables cook particularly well in the microwave and, because fresh vegetables cook in their own moisture, very little additional liquid is necessary. For fresh vegetables, a few tablespoons of water are added, but for most frozen vegetables, no additional liquid is necessary.

Salt sprinkled over vegetables can toughen the vegetables and may cake. It's best to add salt to the water before adding the vegetables or sprinkle on vegetables after microwaving.

TWICE-BAKED POTATOES

4 medium potatoes
1 jar (5 ounces) Neufchâtel cheese spread
    with pimiento
¼ cup milk
2 tablespoons margarine or butter
½ teaspoon salt
    Dash of pepper
    Chopped chives

Prick potatoes in several places with fork. Microwave uncovered on high (100%) 7 minutes; turn over and rearrange potatoes. Microwave until just tender, about 4 minutes. Let stand until cool enough to handle, about 15 minutes.

Cut potatoes lengthwise into halves; scoop out inside, leaving a ¼-inch shell. Mash potatoes until no lumps remain; beat in cheese, milk, margarine, salt and pepper until fluffy. Spoon mixture into potato shells. Sprinkle with chives. Microwave uncovered until hot, 4 to 5 minutes.

8 servings.

CHEESY POTATOES

3 tablespoons margarine or butter
2 tablespoons flour
1 teaspoon salt
¼ teaspoon pepper
1¾ cups milk
1 cup shredded Cheddar cheese (about
    4 ounces)
4 cups ⅛-inch slices potatoes
½ cup chopped green onions
½ teaspoon paprika

Microwave margarine, flour, salt and pepper uncovered in 2½-quart casserole on high (100%) 1 minute; stir until smooth. Microwave until bubbly, 1 minute.

Stir in milk. Cover loosely and microwave until thickened, 5 minutes, stirring every minute. Stir in ¾ cup of the cheese.

Place potatoes and onions in casserole, spooning cheese sauce over potatoes. Cover and

microwave on medium-high (70%) until potatoes are tender, 18 to 20 minutes, turning casserole one-quarter turn every 6 minutes. Mix remaining cheese and the paprika; sprinkle over potatoes. Let stand covered 5 minutes.

8 servings.

HERBED POTATOES

3 or 4 medium potatoes
1 small onion, thinly sliced
2 tablespoons margarine or butter
1 teaspoon dried parsley flakes
½ teaspoon salt
½ teaspoon dried dill weed
¼ teaspoon paprika

Make crosswise cuts ½ inch apart in each potato, not cutting all the way through. Place an onion slice in each cut. Place potatoes in 9-inch pie plate. Cover tightly and microwave on high (100%) until potatoes are almost tender, 4½ to

SAVORY POTATOES

    4 slices bacon, cut into 1-inch pieces
    ½ cup finely chopped green pepper
    ¼ cup finely chopped onion
    ¼ cup bottled Italian dressing
    ½ teaspoon sugar
    ¼ teaspoon celery seed
    1 can (16 ounces) sliced potatoes, drained

Place bacon in 1-quart casserole. Cover loosely and microwave on high (100%) 3 minutes; drain. Mix in green pepper and onion. Cover and microwave until onion is tender, 1 to 2 minutes.

Mix Italian dressing, sugar and celery seed. Carefully fold potatoes and salad dressing mixture into bacon mixture. Cover loosely and microwave until potatoes are hot, 3 to 4 minutes. Sprinkle with paprika if desired.

4 servings.

EASY AU GRATIN POTATO-TOMATO

    2½ cups water
     1 package (5.5 ounces) au gratin
        potatoes
    ⅔ cup milk
     2 tablespoons margarine or butter
     1 can (4 ounces) mushroom stems and
        pieces, drained
     1 to 2 medium tomatoes, chopped
    ½ cup croutons, crushed

Cover and microwave water to boiling in 3-quart casserole on high (100%) 6 to 7 minutes.

Stir in potato slices, Sauce Mix, milk, margarine and mushrooms. Cover and microwave until tender, 15 to 20 minutes. Stir in tomato; top with croutons.

9 servings.

POTATO LOGS

     1 cup water
    ⅓ cup milk
    ½ teaspoon salt
    1⅔ cups instant mashed potatoes
     1 egg, beaten
    ¼ cup finely chopped onion
     2 tablespoons margarine or butter
     2 tablespoons grated Parmesan cheese
     1 teaspoon dried parsley flakes
    ⅓ cup crushed corn flakes

Cover and microwave water, milk and salt to boiling in 4-cup glass measure on high (100%) 3 to 4 minutes. Stir in potatoes; beat in egg. Cool about 30 minutes.

Microwave onion and margarine uncovered in 1-cup glass measure on high (100%) until onion is tender, 3 to 3½ minutes. Stir into cooled potatoes with cheese and parsley flakes.

Shape ⅓ cup potatoes into log about 5 inches long. Roll in corn flakes. Repeat with remaining potatoes. Arrange logs in baking dish. Cover loosely and microwave until hot, 5 to 6 minutes.

6 servings.

CINNAMON SWEET POTATOES

- ½ cup packed brown sugar
- 3 tablespoons margarine or butter
- 2 tablespoons water
- ½ teaspoon salt
- ½ teaspoon ground cinnamon
- 1 can (18 ounces) vacuum-pack sweet potatoes, drained and cut into ½-inch slices

Mix brown sugar, margarine, water and salt in 1-quart casserole. Microwave uncovered on high (100%) until bubbly, about 2 minutes, stirring once.

Stir in sweet potatoes. Cover and microwave 3 minutes; stir potatoes to coat. Cover and microwave until hot, 2 to 4 minutes.

4 servings.

PINEAPPLE-MALLOW SWEET POTATOES

- 1 can (18 ounces) vacuum-pack sweet potatoes
- 1 can (8 ounces) crushed pineapple, drained
- 1 cup miniature marshmallows
- ¼ cup margarine or butter, softened
- 1 teaspoon grated orange peel
- ¼ teaspoon salt
- 1 tablespoon margarine or butter
- ¼ cup packed brown sugar
- ¼ cup chopped pecans or walnuts

Mash potatoes in 1½-quart casserole. Stir in pineapple, marshmallows, ¼ cup margarine, the orange peel and salt.

Microwave 1 tablespoon margarine uncovered in 10-ounce custard cup on high (100%) until melted, 30 seconds to 1 minute. Stir in brown sugar and pecans. Sprinkle over potatoes. Cover and microwave on high (100%) until hot, 6 to 7 minutes.

6 or 7 servings.

CREAMED SPINACH AND MUSHROOMS

- 1 package (10 ounces) frozen chopped spinach
- 2 tablespoons margarine or butter
- 2 cans (4 ounces each) mushroom stems and pieces, drained
- ¼ cup chopped onion
- 1 can (10¾ ounces) condensed cream of mushroom soup
- ¼ teaspoon salt
- ⅛ teaspoon Worcestershire sauce
  Dash of pepper

Microwave frozen spinach in package on high (100%) until thawed, 4 to 5 minutes; drain.

Cover and microwave margarine, mushrooms and onion in 1-quart casserole on high (100%) until onion is crisp-tender, 3 to 4 minutes.

Stir in spinach, soup, salt, Worcestershire sauce and pepper. Cover and microwave 2 minutes; stir. Cover and microwave until hot, 2 to 2½ minutes.

6 servings.

ORIENTAL SPINACH

- 10 to 12 ounces spinach, torn into bite-size pieces
- 1 can (8½ ounces) water chestnuts, drained and sliced
- 5 green onions, sliced
- 2 tablespoons vegetable oil
- 2 tablespoons vinegar
- 2 tablespoons soy sauce
- 1 teaspoon sugar

Cover and microwave spinach, water chestnuts and onions in dish on high (100%) until spinach is limp, 3 to 4 minutes; stir.

Microwave oil, vinegar, soy sauce and sugar to boiling uncovered in 1-cup glass measure, 1 to 1½ minutes. Pour over spinach; toss.

6 servings.

RAISIN-ORANGE ACORN SQUASH

    1 medium acorn squash
    2 tablespoons margarine or butter
  ¼ cup raisins
  ½ teaspoon grated orange peel
  ¼ cup orange juice
    2 tablespoons packed brown sugar
  ¼ teaspoon salt

Prick squash in several places with fork. Microwave on high (100%) 4 minutes; turn squash over. Microwave until just tender, 3 to 5 minutes. Let stand until cool enough to handle, about 15 minutes.

Cut squash lengthwise into halves; remove seeds and fibers. Place squash halves cut sides up in serving dish. Divide margarine, raisins, orange peel, orange juice, brown sugar and salt between squash halves. Cover loosely and microwave on high (100%) until orange juice mixture boils, 4 to 5 minutes.

2 servings.

GOLDEN ORANGE SQUASH BAKE

    2 packages (12 ounces each) frozen
         cooked squash
    2 tablespoons margarine or butter
    1 can (11 ounces) mandarin orange
         segments, drained
  ¼ cup maple-flavored syrup

Place squash and margarine in 2-quart casserole or bowl. Cover loosely and microwave on high (100%) until thawed, 11 to 12 minutes. Top with orange segments; drizzle with syrup. Microwave uncovered until hot, 4 to 5 minutes.

6 servings.

HONEY-CHILI SQUASH

  ¼ cup honey
    2 tablespoons margarine or butter
    1 teaspoon chili powder
  ½ teaspoon salt
    1 package (12 ounces) frozen cooked
         squash, thawed
  ½ cup chopped nuts
  ¼ cup golden raisins

Mix honey, margarine, chili powder and salt in 1-quart casserole. Microwave uncovered on high (100%) until hot and bubbly, 2 to 3 minutes; stir.

Reserve 2 tablespoons of the honey mixture. Stir squash into remaining honey mixture. Toss nuts and raisins with reserved honey mixture; sprinkle over squash. Cover loosely and microwave until squash is hot, 3 to 5 minutes.

4 servings.

Honey-Chili Pumpkin: Substitute 1 can (16 ounces) pumpkin for the squash.

RICE-STUFFED TOMATOES

    6 medium tomatoes
  ⅔ cup instant rice
  ½ cup chopped green onions
    2 tablespoons margarine or butter, melted
    1 teaspoon salt
    1 teaspoon dried basil leaves
  ⅛ teaspoon pepper
    2 tablespoons water

Cut thin slice from stem end of each tomato. Scoop out pulp, leaving a ½-inch wall. Chop pulp; mix with rice, onions, margarine, salt, basil and pepper. Fill tomatoes with rice mixture.

Arrange tomatoes in circle in 9-inch pie plate. Spoon about 1 teaspoon water into each tomato. Cover loosely and microwave on high (100%) 5 minutes; turn pie plate one-half turn. Microwave until tomatoes are hot, 3 to 5 minutes. Sprinkle with Parmesan cheese if desired.

6 servings.

STUFFED TOMATOES

6 medium tomatoes
2 tablespoons margarine or butter
2 tablespoons packed brown sugar
1 slice bread, cubed
½ teaspoon salt
  Dash of pepper

Cut thin slice from stem end of each tomato. Scoop out pulp, leaving a ¼-inch wall; chop enough pulp to measure 1 cup.

Microwave margarine uncovered in 3-cup bowl on high (100%) until melted, 30 seconds to 1 minute. Stir in reserved tomato pulp, the sugar, bread cubes, salt and pepper. Spoon into tomatoes; arrange in circle in 9-inch pie plate. Microwave uncovered on high (100%) until warm, 2½ to 3 minutes.

6 servings.

CHEESE-CRUMBED TOMATOES

2 medium tomatoes
1 tablespoon French dressing
2 tablespoons crushed cheese crackers

Cut tomatoes into halves; arrange cut sides up in circle in 9-inch pie plate. Drizzle cut sides with dressing; sprinkle with crackers. Microwave uncovered on high (100%) 1 minute; turn pie plate one-quarter turn. Microwave until hot, 1½ to 2 minutes.

4 servings.

ZUCCHINI AND CORN

3 medium zucchini, sliced
½ medium green pepper, cut into strips
2 tablespoons water
1 package (10 ounces) frozen corn in butter sauce
¼ teaspoon seasoned salt

Cover and microwave zucchini, green pepper and water in 2-quart casserole or bowl on high (100%) until zucchini is tender, 9 to 10 minutes; drain.

Cut small slit in corn pouch. Microwave corn on high (100%) until hot, 6 to 7 minutes.

Stir corn and salt into zucchini. Microwave uncovered until hot, 1 to 2 minutes.

6 servings.

HARVEST VEGETABLE CASSEROLE

4 small zucchini, cut into ¼-inch slices
1 medium onion, thinly sliced and separated into rings
½ cup finely chopped green pepper
1 clove garlic, finely chopped
1 tablespoon vegetable oil
½ teaspoon salt
⅛ teaspoon pepper
2 medium tomatoes, cut into wedges
  Chopped parsley
  Grated Parmesan cheese

Mix zucchini, onion, green pepper, garlic, oil, salt and pepper in 2-quart casserole. Cover and microwave on high (100%) 3 minutes; stir. Cover and microwave until vegetables are hot but still crisp, 3 to 5 minutes.

Stir in tomatoes. Cover and microwave until tomatoes are hot, 2 to 3 minutes. Sprinkle with parsley and cheese.

8 servings.

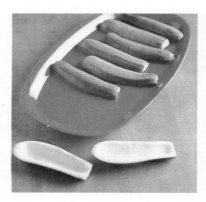

◀ Place the zucchini shells cut sides down on a microwaveproof serving dish. There is no need to add liquid since the zucchini cook in their own moisture.

▶ Microwave reserved zucchini pulp, onions and margarine separately. Then stir in the remaining ingredients and spoon into the cooked shells. Cover loosely and microwave until hot.

For a change-of-pace side dish: Stuffed Zucchini

STUFFED ZUCCHINI

4 medium zucchini
3 green onions, sliced
2 tablespoons margarine or butter
1 slice bread, cubed
¼ cup grated Parmesan cheese
1 medium tomato, chopped
¼ teaspoon salt
   Dash of pepper

Cut zucchini lengthwise into halves. Scoop out pulp, leaving a ¼-inch wall; chop pulp and reserve. Place zucchini shells cut sides down in dish. Cover loosely and microwave on high (100%) until crisp-tender, 5 to 6 minutes.

Cover and microwave reserved pulp, the onions and margarine in 1½-quart casserole or bowl on high (100%) until tender, 6 to 7 minutes. Stir in bread cubes, cheese, tomato, salt and pepper.

Turn zucchini shells cut sides up; spoon mixture into shells. Cover loosely and microwave on high (100%) until hot, 2 to 3 minutes.

8 servings.

NOODLES ROMANOFF

2 cups cooked noodles
1 cup dairy sour cream
2 tablespoons grated Parmesan cheese
2 tablespoons milk
1 tablespoon chopped chives
½ teaspoon salt
¼ teaspoon garlic salt
   Dash of pepper
2 tablespoons grated Parmesan cheese
¼ teaspoon paprika

Mix all ingredients except 2 tablespoons cheese and the paprika in 1-quart casserole. Mix cheese and paprika; sprinkle over noodles. Cover and microwave on high (100%) until hot, 5 to 6 minutes.

4 servings.

BAVARIAN-STYLE MACARONI

5 slices bacon
4 green onions, sliced
2 tablespoons sugar
1 tablespoon flour
1 teaspoon instant beef bouillon
½ teaspoon salt
   Dash of pepper
¼ cup vinegar
½ cup water
1½ cups macaroni, cooked

Place bacon in 1½-quart casserole. Cover loosely and microwave on high (100%) until crisp, 3½ to 4½ minutes. Remove bacon and drain.

Stir green onions, sugar, flour, bouillon, salt, pepper, vinegar and water into bacon fat in casserole. Microwave uncovered until mixture boils and thickens, 3 to 4 minutes.

Stir in macaroni. Crumble bacon; sprinkle over top. Cover and microwave until hot, 3 to 4 minutes.

6 servings.

SPANISH RICE

2 slices bacon, cut into ½-inch pieces
1½ cups instant rice
½ cup chopped green pepper
1⅓ cups water
1 can (16 ounces) stewed tomatoes
1 teaspoon salt
1 teaspoon instant minced onion
½ teaspoon chili powder
¼ teaspoon dried oregano leaves
⅛ teaspoon pepper

Place bacon in 1½-quart casserole. Cover loosely and microwave on high (100%) until crisp, 2 to 3 minutes. Stir in remaining ingredients.

Cover and microwave 5 minutes; stir. Cover and microwave until rice is tender, 5 to 6 minutes.

6 servings.

PARMESAN-BUTTERED ROLLS

¼ cup margarine or butter, softened
2 tablespoons grated Parmesan cheese
1 teaspoon dried parsley flakes
¼ teaspoon garlic salt
6 to 8 dinner rolls

Combine margarine, cheese, parsley flakes and garlic salt. Cut each roll crosswise ⅔ of the way to bottom. Spoon or spread about 1 rounded teaspoon margarine mixture on cut surface of each roll. Microwave uncovered on high (100%) until warm, 30 seconds to 1 minute.

6 to 8 rolls.

MICROWAVE TIPS

Breads heat and cook very quickly. A ring shape is often used to prevent the outside edge from overcooking before the center is cooked. Some bread doughs hold their shape and can be formed into their own ring shape, while others require a special dish with a tube center. You can make your own ring dish by simply placing a straight-sided beverage glass in the center of a round casserole or baking dish.

Though special muffin pans for microwaving are available, you can improvise by placing paper-lined custard or coffee cups in a circle on a large microwavable plate.

ONIONY FRENCH BREAD

⅓ cup margarine or butter, softened
4 green onions, thinly sliced (about
    2 tablespoons)
1 loaf (16 ounces) French bread

Combine margarine and onions. Cut loaf crosswise in half. Slice each horizontally, cutting almost through. Spread cut sides with onion butter. Microwave, one half-loaf at a time, on high (100%) until hot, 45 seconds to 1 minute. Cut into serving pieces.

CORN MUFFINS

½ cup buttermilk baking mix
¼ cup yellow cornmeal
2 teaspoons sugar
⅛ teaspoon salt
¼ cup milk
2 teaspoons vegetable oil
1 egg
   Corn flakes, crushed

Mix baking mix, cornmeal, sugar and salt. Beat milk, oil and egg. Stir into dry ingredients just until moistened. Spoon into 5 paper-lined plastic muffin cups or custard cups, filling ½ full. (If using custard cups, arrange in circle on 12-inch plate.) Sprinkle lightly with corn flakes.

Microwave uncovered on high (100%) 1½ minutes; turn one-half turn and microwave until no longer doughy, 30 seconds to 1 minute. Immediately remove from cups.

5 muffins.

ORANGE-OATMEAL MUFFINS

1 egg
¾ cup buttermilk
½ cup vegetable oil
2 tablespoons finely shredded orange peel
1 cup whole wheat flour
1 cup quick-cooking oats
¼ cup packed brown sugar
2 teaspoons baking powder
½ teaspoon baking soda
½ teaspoon salt

Beat egg; stir in buttermilk, oil and orange peel. Stir in remaining ingredients just until moistened. (Batter will be lumpy.) Spoon half of the batter into 6 paper-lined plastic muffin cups or custard cups, filling ½ full. (If using custard cups, arrange in circle on 12-inch plate.)

Microwave uncovered on high (100%) 1 minute; turn one-half turn and microwave until wooden pick inserted in center comes out clean, 1½ to 2½ minutes. (Edges of muffins will look moist.) Let stand 1 minute; remove from cups. Repeat with remaining batter.

12 muffins.

CARAMEL BISCUIT RING

¼ cup margarine or butter
⅓ cup packed brown sugar
1 tablespoon corn syrup
¼ cup chopped nuts
1½ cups buttermilk baking mix
⅓ cup water

Microwave margarine, brown sugar and corn syrup uncovered in round baking dish, 8 x 1½ inches, on high (100%) 1 minute; stir. Microwave until bubbly, 1 to 1½ minutes. Stir in nuts.

Mix baking mix and water. Drop dough by 7 spoonfuls around side of baking dish, forming a ring. Spoon some of the caramel mixture from center over each biscuit.

Cover loosely and microwave 1½ minutes; turn dish one-quarter turn. Microwave until no longer doughy, 30 seconds to 1 minute. Immediately invert on serving plate; leave dish over biscuits 2 minutes.

7 servings.

CINNAMON-SUGAR BLUEBERRY MUFFINS

1 package (13.5 ounces) wild blueberry muffin mix
½ cup milk
1 egg
2 tablespoons margarine or butter
3 tablespoons sugar
½ teaspoon ground cinnamon

Prepare muffin mix batter as directed on package. Spoon into 6 paper-lined plastic muffin cups or custard cups, filling ½ full. (If using custard cups, arrange in circle on 12-inch plate.)

Microwave uncovered on high (100%) 1½ minutes; turn one-half turn and microwave until no longer doughy, 30 seconds to 1 minute. Immediately remove from cups. Repeat with remaining batter.

Microwave margarine uncovered in small dish on high (100%) until melted, 30 seconds to 1 minute. Mix sugar and cinnamon. Dip tops of muffins in melted margarine, then in cinnamon-sugar mixture.

12 muffins.

FRENCH BREAKFAST PUFFS

⅔ cup all-purpose flour
⅓ cup sugar
¼ cup milk
 3 tablespoons vegetable oil
 1 egg
¾ teaspoon baking powder
¼ teaspoon salt
⅛ teaspoon ground nutmeg
 2 tablespoons margarine or butter
 3 tablespoons sugar
¼ teaspoon ground cinnamon

Mix flour, ⅓ cup sugar, the milk, oil, egg, baking powder, salt and nutmeg until smooth. Spoon into 5 paper-lined custard cups; arrange in circle on 12-inch plate.

Microwave uncovered on high (100%) 1½ minutes; turn plate one-half turn and microwave until wooden pick inserted in center comes out clean, 30 seconds to 1½ minutes. (Parts of puffs will look moist.) Immediately remove from cups.

Microwave margarine uncovered in small dish until melted, 30 seconds to 1 minute. Mix 3 tablespoons sugar and the cinnamon. Dip tops in melted margarine, then in cinnamon-sugar mixture.

5 puffs.

BANANA STICKY BUNS

½ cup packed brown sugar
½ cup margarine or butter
½ cup chopped walnuts
 2 cups buttermilk baking mix
⅔ cup mashed ripe bananas
 2 tablespoons margarine or butter, softened
¼ cup packed brown sugar

Microwave ½ cup brown sugar, ½ cup margarine and the walnuts uncovered in square baking dish, 8 x 8 x 2 inches, on high (100%) until bubbly and sugar is dissolved, 1½ to 2 minutes, stirring occasionally.

Mix baking mix and bananas until a soft dough forms. Gently smooth dough into a ball on floured cloth-covered board. Knead 5 times. Roll dough into rectangle, 15 x 9 inches. Spread with 2 tablespoons margarine; sprinkle with ¼ cup brown sugar. Roll up, beginning at wide side. Pinch edge of dough into roll to seal well. Cut into twelve 1¼-inch slices. Place slices cut sides down in baking dish.

Microwave uncovered on high (100%) 2 minutes; turn dish one-quarter turn and microwave until no longer doughy, about 3 minutes. Immediately invert on cookie sheet; leave dish over buns 1 minute.

12 buns.

DESSERTS

FRUIT AND DUMPLINGS

 1 package (10 ounces) frozen raspberries,
      thawed
 1 can (16 ounces) sliced pears
 2 tablespoons cornstarch
 1 teaspoon ground cinnamon
 ⅓ cup sugar
 ¾ cup buttermilk baking mix
 2 tablespoons sugar
 ¼ cup dairy sour cream
 1 egg

Drain syrups from fruits into 4-cup glass measure; add enough water to measure 1½ cups. Stir in cornstarch, cinnamon and ⅓ cup sugar. Microwave uncovered on high (100%) 2 minutes; stir. Microwave until mixture boils and thickens, 2 to 3 minutes. Combine with fruits in round baking dish, 8 x 1½ inches.

Mix baking mix, 2 tablespoons sugar, the sour cream and egg; spoon onto fruit mixture, forming a ring around side of baking dish. (Topping will cook toward center.) Spoon some of fruit sauce over topping. Microwave uncovered on high (100%) 3 minutes; turn dish one-quarter turn. Microwave until topping is no longer doughy, 3½ to 4½ minutes.

5 or 6 servings.

CRUNCHY BLUEBERRY DELIGHT

 ½ cup margarine or butter
1⅓ cups flaked coconut
 1 cup all-purpose flour
 ¾ cup packed brown sugar
 ⅔ cup graham cracker crumbs (about
      9 squares)
 1 package (20 ounces) frozen
      unsweetened blueberries (about
      4 cups)
 ¾ cup granulated sugar
 3 tablespoons cornstarch
 ½ cup water

Microwave margarine uncovered in square baking dish, 8 x 8 x 2 inches, on high (100%) until melted, 30 seconds to 1 minute. Stir in coconut, flour, brown sugar and cracker crumbs. Microwave until lightly toasted, 5 to 7 minutes, stirring every 2 minutes. Reserve ¾ cup coconut mixture for topping; press remaining mixture fimly and evenly in baking dish.

Mix blueberries, granulated sugar and cornstarch in 2-quart casserole or bowl. Gradually stir in water. Cover and microwave on high (100%) until mixture boils and thickens, 11 to 12 minutes, stirring every 4 minutes. Cool slightly.

Spoon blueberries over coconut crust. Sprinkle with reserved coconut mixture. Refrigerate until set, 2 to 4 hours. Cut into squares.

9 servings.

EASY POACHED PEARS

 4 fresh pears, cut into halves and cored
 1 orange, pared and sectioned
 2 tablespoons margarine or butter
⅓ cup honey
⅓ cup sweet white wine
 1 package (3 ounces) cream cheese
   Ground nutmeg

Arrange pear halves cut sides up in oblong baking dish, 12 x 7½ x 2 inches. Place an orange section in each pear half. Dot each with margarine; drizzle with honey and wine. Cover loosely and microwave on high (100%) 3 minutes; turn dish one-half turn. Microwave until pears are tender, 3 to 4 minutes.

Microwave cream cheese uncovered in bowl on high (100%) until softened, about 30 seconds. Beat until fluffy. Spoon onto each pear half; sprinkle with nutmeg.

8 servings.

SUGAR-BAKED APPLES

⅔ cup sugar
⅓ cup all-purpose flour
 1 teaspoon ground cinnamon
¼ cup margarine or butter
 2 tablespoons raisins
 4 cooking apples, cut into halves and cored
⅓ cup orange juice

Mix sugar, flour and cinnamon; cut in margarine until crumbly. Stir in raisins.

Arrange apples cut sides up in round baking dish, 8 x 1½ inches. Spoon crumb mixture over apples. Drizzle with orange juice. Cover loosely and microwave on high (100%) 4½ minutes; turn dish one-quarter turn. Microwave until apples are tender, 2½ to 3½ minutes.

8 servings.

APPLE CRUMB DESSERT

 4 cups sliced pared apples (about
   4 medium)
½ teaspoon ground cinnamon
 1 cup all-purpose flour
¼ cup granulated sugar
¼ cup packed brown sugar
¼ teaspoon salt
¼ teaspoon baking soda
 1 egg
¼ cup packed brown sugar
⅓ cup margarine or butter

Arrange apples in square baking dish, 8 x 8 x 2 inches. Sprinkle with cinnamon. Mix flour, granulated sugar, ¼ cup brown sugar, the salt, baking soda and egg with fork until crumbly. Spoon over apples. Sprinkle with ¼ cup brown sugar.

Microwave margarine uncovered in 1-cup glass measure on high (100%) until melted, 30 seconds to 1 minute; drizzle over apples. Microwave uncovered on high (100%) until apples are tender, 10 to 12 minutes. Serve warm and, if desired, with cream.

6 servings.

Pictured at right: A choice of old-fashioned desserts. Clockwise from top — Meringue-topped Rice Pudding (page 69), Peanut Butter Bars (page 83) and Sugar-baked Apples (this page).

SWEETENED HOT GRAPEFRUIT

2 grapefruit
4 tablespoons packed brown sugar or
      honey
4 teaspoons sweet white wine or grenadine
      syrup (optional)

Cut grapefruit into halves; remove seeds. Cut around edges and sections to loosen; remove centers. Sprinkle each half with 1 tablespoon brown sugar and 1 teaspoon wine. Place grapefruit in serving dishes. Microwave uncovered on high (100%) until hot, 4 to 6 minutes.

4 servings.

REFRESHING RHUBARB DESSERT

½ cup margarine or butter
1 cup rolled oats
¾ cup all-purpose flour
⅔ cup packed brown sugar
1 teaspoon ground cinnamon
4 cups sliced rhubarb
1 cup granulated sugar
¾ cup orange juice
2 tablespoons cornstarch

Microwave margarine uncovered in round baking dish, 8 x 1½ inches, on high (100%) until melted, 30 seconds to 1 minute. Stir in oats, flour, brown sugar and cinnamon. Microwave 1 minute; stir. Microwave until well coated, 1 to 1½ minutes. Reserve half of the oat mixture; press remaining mixture firmly and evenly in baking dish. Add rhubarb.

Mix granulated sugar, orange juice and cornstarch in 4-cup glass measure. Microwave uncovered on high (100%) 1 minute; stir. Microwave to boiling, 1 to 2 minutes. Pour over rhubarb. Sprinkle with reserved oat mixture. Microwave uncovered on high (100%) until rhubarb is tender, 7 to 8 minutes; cool.

6 to 8 servings.

RHUBARB CRUNCH

4 cups sliced fresh rhubarb (about
      1 pound)
1 cup sugar
⅛ teaspoon almond extract
¼ cup margarine or butter
4 slices bread, cut into ¼-inch cubes
¼ cup sugar
½ cup chopped almonds
1 teaspoon grated orange peel

Mix rhubarb and 1 cup sugar in 2½-quart casserole. Cover and microwave on high (100%) until rhubarb is tender, 7 to 9 minutes. Stir in almond extract. Cool rhubarb sauce.

Microwave margarine uncovered in 10-inch pie plate on high (100%) until melted, 30 seconds to 1 minute. Stir in bread cubes, ¼ cup sugar and the almonds until well coated with margarine. Microwave until toasted, 7 to 8 minutes, stirring every 2 minutes. Stir in orange peel. To serve, spoon rhubarb sauce into dessert dishes; top with toasted bread mixture.

6 servings.

Applesauce Crunch: Substitute 2½ to 3 cups applesauce for the cooked rhubarb sauce.

MICROWAVE TIP

Brown sugar and spices like nutmeg and cinnamon do double duty for microwaved desserts. Each gives its own special flavoring and, at the same time, adds a dash of color. This is particularly welcome for those dishes that would have a brown appearance when baked in a conventional oven.

MERINGUE-TOPPED RICE PUDDING

1 package (3⅛ ounces) vanilla regular pudding and pie filling
½ cup uncooked instant rice
½ cup raisins
3 cups milk
2 eggs, separated
¼ teaspoon cream of tartar
¼ cup sugar
½ teaspoon vanilla
　Ground nutmeg

Mix pudding and pie filling (dry), rice, raisins and milk in 1½-quart casserole. Cover and microwave on high (100%) 4 minutes; stir. Microwave uncovered to boiling, 3½ to 4½ minutes.

Beat egg yolks; gradually beat in about 1 cup of the hot pudding. Blend into pudding in casserole. Microwave uncovered just until edges are bubbly, 1 to 1½ minutes. Cool 10 minutes.

Beat egg whites and cream of tartar until foamy. Beat in sugar, 1 tablespoon at a time; continue beating until stiff peaks form. Beat in vanilla. Spoon meringue onto pudding in 6 to 8 mounds. Microwave uncovered until meringue is set, 2 to 2½ minutes. Sprinkle with nutmeg.

6 to 8 servings.

DELUXE BREAD PUDDING

2 tablespoons margarine or butter
⅓ cup packed brown sugar
½ teaspoon ground cinnamon
4 slices bread
⅓ cup raisins
1¾ cups milk
3 eggs, slightly beaten
¼ cup granulated sugar
¼ teaspoon salt
1 teaspoon vanilla
　Ground cinnamon

Microwave margarine uncovered in 1-cup glass measure on high (100%) until softened, 15 to 30 seconds. Stir in brown sugar and ½ teaspoon cinnamon. Spread 2 slices bread with brown sugar mixture. Top each slice with second slice, making 2 sandwiches. Cut each sandwich into nine 1-inch squares. Layer squares in 1-quart casserole. Sprinkle with raisins.

Microwave milk uncovered in 4-cup glass measure on high (100%) until steaming hot, about 3½ minutes. Beat in eggs, granulated sugar, salt and vanilla gradually. Pour over bread mixture; sprinkle with cinnamon.

Place casserole in square baking dish, 8 x 8 x 2 inches. Pour 1 cup hot water into dish. Microwave uncovered on high (100%) until knife inserted near center comes out clean, 8 to 10 minutes. Let stand in baking dish with water at least 10 minutes.

4 to 6 servings.

MINCEMEAT STEAMED PUDDING

    2 tablespoons margarine or butter,
       softened
    ½ cup packed brown sugar
    2 eggs
    1 cup prepared mincemeat
    ⅓ cup milk
 1 ¼ cups all-purpose flour
 1 ½ teaspoons baking powder
    ½ cup chopped nuts
       Rum Sauce (right)

Grease 6-cup ring dish. Mix margarine, brown sugar and eggs. Stir in mincemeat and milk. Mix in flour, baking powder and nuts. Spoon batter into dish. Cover tightly with plastic wrap.

Microwave on inverted dinner plate on high (100%) until no longer doughy, 6 to 7 minutes, rotating dish every 2 minutes. Cool 5 minutes. Uncover and invert pudding onto serving plate. Serve with Rum Sauce.

8 to 10 servings.

RUM SAUCE
    ¾ cup whipping cream
    ¼ cup milk
    ¾ cup sugar
    1 tablespoon cornstarch
    ½ cup margarine or butter
    1 teaspoon rum flavoring or 1 tablespoon
       rum

Mix whipping cream, milk, sugar and cornstarch in 4-cup glass measure. Add margarine. Microwave uncovered on high (100%) 3 minutes; stir. Microwave to boiling, 1 to 2 minutes. Stir in rum.

For a special holiday treat: Mincemeat Steamed Pudding

FRUIT STREUSEL PUDDING CAKE

1   can (21 ounces) cherry pie filling
1   can (8¾ ounces) sliced peaches
½   package (18.5-ounce size) yellow cake mix
      with pudding (about 2 cups)
½   cup chopped nuts
½   teaspoon ground cinnamon
⅓   cup margarine or butter

Mix pie filling and peaches (with syrup) in 2-quart casserole. Sprinkle cake mix (dry), nuts and cinnamon onto fruit mixture.

Microwave margarine uncovered in 1-cup glass measure on high (100%) until melted, 30 seconds to 1 minute; drizzle over topping. Microwave uncovered on high (100%) until bubbly and topping is almost firm, 11 to 13 minutes, rotating casserole every 4 minutes.

6 to 8 servings.

CHOCOLATE-CREAM CAKE DESSERT

½   package (18.5-ounce size) yellow cake mix
      with pudding (about 2 cups)
½   cup water
2   tablespoons vegetable oil
1   egg
⅔   cup sugar
1   envelope unflavored gelatin
⅛   teaspoon salt
1¼ cups milk
2   squares (1 ounce each) unsweetened
      chocolate
2   eggs, beaten
1   teaspoon vanilla
1   cup chilled whipping cream

Grease bottom only of oblong baking dish, 12 x 7½ x 2 inches. Beat cake mix, water, oil and egg in large mixer bowl on low speed until moistened. Beat on medium speed 2 minutes. Pour batter into baking dish; spread evenly. Microwave uncovered on high (100%) 4 minutes; turn dish one-half turn. Microwave until

wooden pick inserted near center comes out clean, 2½ to 3½ minutes. (Parts of the cake will appear very moist, but these parts will continue to cook while standing.) Cool thoroughly. Cut into 1-inch squares.

Mix sugar, gelatin and salt in 2-quart casserole or bowl. Gradually stir in milk. Add chocolate. Microwave uncovered on high (100%) to boiling, 4 to 5 minutes, stirring every 2 minutes. Beat until mixture is smooth.

Gradually stir a small amount of the hot mixture into eggs. Blend into hot mixture in casserole. Stir in vanilla; cool.

Beat whipping cream in 4-quart bowl until very soft peaks form. Fold in chocolate mixture; then fold in cake squares. Spoon into dessert dishes. Refrigerate until set, at least 2 hours.

12 servings.

ICE CREAM WITH BUTTERSCOTCH SAUCE

⅔   cup packed brown sugar
⅓   cup corn syrup
¼   cup margarine or butter
¼   cup milk
½   teaspoon vanilla
      Ice cream (vanilla, butter pecan, coffee)

Mix brown sugar, corn syrup, margarine and milk in 4-cup glass measure. Microwave uncovered on high (100%) 1½ minutes; stir. Microwave to a rapid boil, 1 to 1½ minutes. Stir in vanilla. Serve over ice cream. Cover and refrigerate any leftover sauce. To reheat, microwave until warm, 1 to 1½ minutes.

1¼ cups sauce.

ICE CREAM WITH RUM SAUCE

½ cup margarine or butter
1 cup sugar
1 can (5⅓ ounces) evaporated milk
1 teaspoon ground nutmeg
2 tablespoons rum or 1 teaspoon rum
   flavoring
   Ice cream

Mix all ingredients except rum and ice cream in 4-cup glass measure. Microwave uncovered on high (100%) 3½ minutes, stirring after each minute. Stir in rum. Serve warm over ice cream.

About 1½ cups sauce.

FROZEN RASPBERRY SQUARES

⅓ cup margarine or butter
1 cup all-purpose flour
¼ cup packed brown sugar
1 pint raspberry sherbet
1 quart vanilla ice cream
1 package (10 ounces) frozen raspberries,
   thawed
2 tablespoons granulated sugar
1 tablespoon cornstarch

Microwave margarine uncovered in square baking dish, 8 x 8 x 2 inches, on high (100%) until melted, 30 seconds to 1 minute. Stir in flour and brown sugar. Microwave until light brown, 3 to 4 minutes, stirring every minute. Reserve ⅓ cup crumb mixture for topping; press remaining mixture firmly and evenly in baking dish. Cool.

Spoon and spread sherbet in one layer on crumb crust; top with ice cream layer. Sprinkle with reserved crumb mixture. Cover and freeze until firm, at least 6 to 8 hours.

Drain liquid from raspberries into 2-cup glass measure; add enough water to measure 1 cup. Stir in granulated sugar and cornstarch. Microwave uncovered on high (100%) 2 minutes; stir. Microwave to boiling, 30 seconds to 1½ minutes. Stir in raspberries. Refrigerate until ready to serve. Cut dessert into squares; serve with raspberry sauce.

9 servings.

CHOCO-MINT DESSERT SQUARES

2 tablespoons margarine or butter
13 creme-filled chocolate cookies, finely
   crushed (about 1⅓ cups)
1 cup boiling water
1 package (3 ounces) lime-flavored
   gelatin
1 package (8 ounces) cream cheese
¾ cup sugar
2 or 3 drops green food color (optional)
1 cup whipping cream, whipped
¾ cup chocolate-flavored ice-cream
   topping
½ teaspoon peppermint extract

Microwave margarine uncovered in oblong baking dish, 12 x 7½ x 2 inches, on high (100%) until melted, 30 seconds to 1 minute. Stir in cookie crumbs. Press mixture firmly and evenly in baking dish; refrigerate.

Pour boiling water over gelatin, stirring until gelatin is dissolved. Cool 30 minutes.

Microwave cream cheese uncovered in 2½-quart casserole or bowl on high (100%) until softened, 45 seconds to 1 minute. Beat in sugar until smooth. Gradually beat in gelatin mixture and food color. Fold in whipped cream. Pour over crumb crust. Refrigerate until set, at least 4 hours.

Combine ice-cream topping and peppermint extract. Cut dessert into squares; serve with chocolate sauce.

15 servings.

PUMPKIN SQUARES

¼ cup margarine or butter
½ cup all-purpose flour
¼ cup packed brown sugar
¼ cup rolled oats
1 envelope unflavored gelatin
¼ cup cold water
1 can (16 ounces) pumpkin
2 eggs
1 cup evaporated milk
¾ cup packed brown sugar
1 teaspoon ground cinnamon
½ teaspoon salt
¼ teaspoon ground ginger
¼ teaspoon ground cloves
   Whipped cream

Microwave margarine uncovered in square baking dish, 8 x 8 x 2 inches, on high (100%) until melted, 30 seconds to 1 minute. Stir in flour, ¼ cup brown sugar and the oats. Microwave 1½ minutes; stir. Microwave until light brown, 1½ to 2 minutes. Press mixture firmly and evenly in baking dish.

Sprinkle gelatin on cold water in 2½-quart casserole or bowl to soften. Beat in pumpkin, eggs, evaporated milk, ¾ cup brown sugar, the cinnamon, salt, ginger and cloves. Microwave uncovered on high (100%) 4 minutes; stir. Microwave until thickened, 4 to 4½ minutes, stirring every minute. Pour onto crust.

Microwave uncovered on high (100%) 2 minutes; turn dish one-quarter turn. Microwave 3 minutes. Refrigerate until set, 2 to 3 hours. Serve with whipped cream.

9 servings.

MOCHA FROZEN CREME

⅓ cup milk
1 teaspoon instant coffee
1 cup miniature marshmallows
½ cup semisweet chocolate chips
¼ cup chopped almonds
1 tablespoon brandy (optional)
½ teaspoon vanilla
1 cup chilled whipping cream
2 tablespoons sugar

Mix milk and coffee in 4-cup glass measure. Add marshmallows and chocolate chips. Microwave uncovered on high (100%) to boiling, 1½ to 2 minutes; stir until smooth. Stir in almonds, brandy and vanilla; cool.

Beat whipping cream and sugar in chilled bowl until stiff. Fold chocolate mixture into whipped cream. Spoon into 8 paper-lined muffin cups. Freeze until firm, about 4 hours. To serve, peel off papers and, if desired, top each with additional whipped cream and a maraschino cherry.

8 servings.

MICROWAVED PIE SHELL

Prepare pastry for 9-inch One-Crust Pie as directed on package of pie crust sticks or mix except—prick bottom and side with fork. Microwave uncovered on high (100%) 2 minutes; turn pie plate one-half turn. Microwave until crust has a dry, flaky appearance, 2 to 3 minutes.

PECAN TARTS

    3 eggs
    1 cup sugar
    1 cup corn syrup
   ⅓ cup margarine or butter
   ½ cup chopped pecans
    1 teaspoon vanilla
    2 packages (5 ounces each) baked pastry
       shells (3-inch size)
       Whipped cream (optional)

Beat eggs, sugar and corn syrup in 2-quart casserole or bowl. Add margarine and pecans. Microwave uncovered on high (100%) until mixture boils and thickens slightly, 5 to 7 minutes, stirring every 2 minutes. Stir in vanilla.

Remove pastry shells from foil pans; place 6 shells on a plate. Pour filling into shells. Microwave uncovered on high (100%), one plate at a time, until filling starts to bubble, 30 seconds to 1 minute. Refrigerate until ready to serve. Top with whipped cream.

12 tarts.

STRAWBERRY-RHUBARB PIE

  1½ cups all-purpose flour
   ½ teaspoon salt
   ½ cup shortening
    3 to 4 tablespoons cold water
    3 cups ¼-inch slices rhubarb
    1 pint fresh strawberries, cut into halves
  1⅓ cups sugar
   ¼ cup cornstarch
    2 tablespoons margarine or butter

Mix flour and salt; cut in shortening thoroughly. Sprinkle in water, 1 tablespoon at a time, mixing until flour is moistened and pastry almost cleans side of bowl.

Gather pastry into a ball. Reserve ¼ of the pastry; shape remaining pastry into flattened round on lightly floured cloth-covered board. Roll 2 inches larger than inverted 9-inch pie plate. Fold pastry into quarters; place in pie plate. Unfold pastry and ease into plate. Trim over-hanging edge of pastry 1 inch from rim of plate. Fold and roll pastry under, even with plate; flute. Prick bottom and side thoroughly with fork.

Microwave uncovered on high (100%) 2½ minutes; turn pie plate one-quarter turn. Microwave until crust has a dry, flaky appearance, 1½ to 2½ minutes.

Roll reserved pastry to 8-inch circle; place on plate. Cut into 6 or 8 wedges. If desired, sprinkle with about 1 teaspoon cinnamon-sugar. Microwave uncovered on high (100%) until crust has a dry, flaky appearance, 2 to 3 minutes; cool.

Mix remaining ingredients in 2-quart casserole. Cover and microwave on high (100%) 5 minutes; stir. Microwave uncovered until mixture boils and thickens, 6 to 8 minutes, stirring every 2 minutes. Cool slightly, about 30 minutes. Pour into pie shell; top with pastry wedges. Cool. Serve with ice cream if desired.

PUMPKIN MERINGUE PIE

9 - inch Microwaved Pie Shell (page 74)
2 eggs, separated
1 can (13 ounces) evaporated milk (about 1⅔ cups)
1 package (4½ ounces) egg custard mix
1 can (16 ounces) pumpkin
¼ cup packed brown sugar
¾ teaspoon ground cinnamon
¼ teaspoon ground nutmeg
¼ teaspoon ground cloves
⅛ teaspoon ground ginger
¼ teaspoon cream of tartar
¼ cup granulated sugar

Prepare and microwave pie shell. Beat egg yolks in 2½-quart casserole or bowl. Beat in remaining ingredients except egg whites, cream of tartar and granulated sugar. Microwave uncovered on high (100%) to boiling, 7 to 8 minutes, stirring every 2 minutes. Pour into pie shell.

Beat egg whites and cream of tartar until foamy. Beat in granulated sugar, 1 tablespoon at a time, until stiff peaks form. Spread meringue around edge of pie. Microwave uncovered on high (100%) until meringue is set, 1½ to 2 minutes. Refrigerate until set, at least 4 hours.

PEACHES AND CREAM PIE

9 - inch Microwaved Pie Shell (page 74)
3 tablespoons cornstarch
¾ cup sugar
1½ cups water
1 package (3 ounces) peach-flavored gelatin
½ teaspoon almond extract
2 cups sliced peaches (about 4 medium)*
2 cups sweetened whipped cream or whipped topping

Prepare and microwave pie shell. Mix cornstarch, sugar and water in 1-quart casserole or bowl. Microwave uncovered on high (100%)

2 minutes; stir. Microwave until mixture boils and thickens, 2 to 2½ minutes. Stir in gelatin and extract. Cool 30 minutes.

Arrange peaches in pie shell. Top with gelatin mixture. Refrigerate until set, 3 to 4 hours. Just before serving, top pie with whipped cream.

*1 can (16 ounces) peach slices, drained, can be substituted for the fresh peaches. Use drained syrup for part of the water.

BLUEBERRY CREAM PIE

9 - inch Microwaved Pie Shell (page 74)
1 package (20 ounces) frozen blueberries (about 4 cups)
¾ cup sugar
3 tablespoons cornstarch
½ cup water
1 package (8 ounces) cream cheese
1 container (9 ounces) frozen whipped topping, thawed (about 4 cups)

Prepare and microwave pie shell. Combine frozen blueberries and sugar in 1-quart casserole or bowl. Cover and microwave on high (100%) 2 minutes; stir. Cover and microwave until berries are thawed, 2 to 3 minutes.

Mix cornstarch and water in 2-cup glass measure. Spoon in juice from berries. Microwave uncovered on high (100%) 1 minute; stir. Microwave until mixture boils and thickens, 1 to 1½ minutes. Stir into berries; cool 15 minutes.

Microwave cream cheese uncovered in 2½-quart casserole or bowl on high (100%) until softened, 45 seconds to 1 minute. Beat until smooth. Reserve 1 cup of the berry mixture; fold remainder into cream cheese. Stir in whipped topping. Spoon into pie shell. Top with reserved berry mixture. Refrigerate until set, 2 to 3 hours.

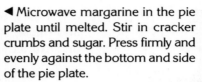

◄ Microwave margarine in the pie plate until melted. Stir in cracker crumbs and sugar. Press firmly and evenly against the bottom and side of the pie plate.

► The chocolate chips will retain their shape during microwaving so they must be stirred to achieve a smooth consistency.

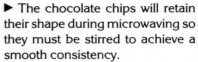

◄ Let chocolate mixture stand without covering 10 minutes to cool. (Letting food stand covered after microwaving is a method of allowing for additional cooking.)

► Caramel candies soften rapidly and lose their shape when microwaved. However, stirring is still needed for smooth consistency.

The grand finale: Frosty Chocolate-Caramel Pie garnished with dollops of whipped topping

FROSTY CHOCOLATE-CARAMEL PIE

Graham Cracker Crust (below)
1 package (6 ounces) semisweet
   chocolate chips
3 tablespoons water
1 teaspoon vanilla
1 container (8 ounces) frozen whipped
   topping, thawed (about 4 cups)
28 caramel candies
¼ cup water
⅓ cup pecan halves

Prepare and microwave Graham Cracker Crust. Microwave chocolate chips and 3 tablespoons water uncovered in 2½-quart bowl or casserole on high (100%) until chocolate is softened, 1 to 1½ minutes. Stir until smooth; let stand 10 minutes. Stir in vanilla; fold in whipped topping. Spoon into crust. Freeze until firm, at least 4 hours.

Microwave caramel candies and ¼ cup water uncovered in 2-cup glass measure on high (100%) until candies are softened, 1½ to 2½ minutes. Stir until smooth. Stir in pecans; cool. Serve over pie.

GRAHAM CRACKER CRUST
¼ cup margarine or butter
1¼ cups graham cracker crumbs
   (about 15 squares)
2 tablespoons sugar

Microwave margarine uncovered in 9-inch pie plate on high (100%) until melted, 30 seconds to 1 minute. Stir in graham cracker crumbs and sugar. Press mixture firmly against bottom and up side of pie plate. Microwave uncovered 45 seconds; turn pie plate one-quarter turn. Microwave until lightly browned, 45 seconds to 1½ minutes.

IMPOSSIBLE FRENCH APPLE PIE

6 cups sliced pared tart apples
1¼ teaspoon ground cinnamon
¼ teaspoon ground nutmeg
½ cup milk
2 tablespoons margarine or butter,
   softened
2 eggs
1 cup sugar
⅓ cup buttermilk baking mix
   Streusel Topping (below)
   Ground cinnamon (optional)

Grease 10-inch pie plate. Mix apples, 1¼ teaspoons cinnamon and the nutmeg; turn into pie plate. Beat remaining ingredients except Streusel Topping and cinnamon until smooth, 15 seconds in blender on high or 1 minute with hand beater. Pour over apples. Sprinkle with Streusel Topping and cinnamon.

Microwave uncovered on medium-high (70%) until knife inserted in center comes out clean, 24 to 28 minutes, turning pie plate one-quarter turn every 8 minutes. Cool on flat, heatproof surface.

STREUSEL TOPPING
1 cup buttermilk baking mix
½ cup chopped nuts
⅓ cup packed brown sugar
2 tablespoons firm margarine or butter

Mix all ingredients until crumbly.

CARROT CAKE

¼ cup graham cracker crumbs
3 cups buttermilk baking mix
2½ cups lightly packed shredded carrots
1 cup packed brown sugar
1 cup chopped nuts
1 cup vegetable oil
1 tablespoon ground cinnamon
2 teaspoons ground nutmeg
1 teaspoon vanilla
4 eggs
Cream Cheese Glaze (below)

Generously grease 12-cup bundt cake dish; sprinkle with graham cracker crumbs. Blend remaining ingredients except Cream Cheese Glaze in large mixer bowl on low speed, scraping bowl constantly. Beat 2 minutes on medium speed, scraping bowl occasionally. Pour batter into cake dish.

Microwave uncovered on inverted dinner plate on high (100%) until cake pulls away from sides of dish and surface is almost dry, 10 to 14 minutes, turning dish one-quarter turn every 4 minutes. Immediately invert on heatproof serving plate; remove dish. Cool cake thoroughly. Spread with Cream Cheese Glaze and, if desired, sprinkle with chopped nuts. Store tightly covered.

CREAM CHEESE GLAZE
Mix 1 package (3 ounces) cream cheese, softened, 1 cup powdered sugar and 1 to 2 teaspoons milk until smooth and of desired consistency.

CHOCOLATE MACAROON CAKE

1 cup all-purpose flour
¾ cup sugar
¼ cup unsweetened cocoa
½ teaspoon baking soda
¼ teaspoon salt
½ teaspoon vanilla
¼ cup shortening
¾ cup buttermilk
1 egg
Macaroon Filling (below)
Chocolate Frosting (below)

Grease bottom only of oblong baking dish, 10 x 6 x 1½ inches. Blend all ingredients except Macaroon Filling and Chocolate Frosting in large mixer bowl on low speed, scraping bowl constantly. Beat 3 minutes on high speed, scraping bowl occasionally. Pour batter evenly into baking dish. Spoon Macaroon Filling onto batter by teaspoonfuls.

Microwave uncovered on high (100%) 5 minutes; turn dish one-half turn. Microwave until wooden pick inserted in center comes out clean, 3 to 4 minutes. (Parts of the cake will appear very moist, but these parts will continue to cook while standing.) Cool thoroughly; frost with Chocolate Frosting.

MACAROON FILLING
1 cup flaked or grated coconut
¼ cup corn syrup
1 tablespoon flour
1 tablespoon milk
½ teaspoon almond extract

Mix all ingredients.

CHOCOLATE FROSTING
2 cups powdered sugar
2 tablespoons unsweetened cocoa
3 tablespoons margarine or butter, softened
½ teaspoon vanilla
2 or 3 tablespoons milk or water

Mix powdered sugar, cocoa and margarine. Stir in vanilla. Beat in milk, 1 teaspoon at a time, until smooth and of spreading consistency.

APPLESAUCE RAISIN UPSIDE-DOWN CAKE

⅓ cup packed brown sugar
¼ cup chopped nuts
3 tablespoons margarine or butter
1 package (13.5 ounces) applesauce
    raisin cake mix
1 cup water

Microwave brown sugar, nuts and margarine uncovered in round baking dish, 8 x 1½ inches, on high (100%) until margarine is melted, 1 to 1½ minutes; stir. Microwave to boiling, 1 to 1½ minutes. Spread evenly in baking dish.

Mix cake mix and water until smooth; pour over nut mixture in baking dish. Microwave uncovered 5 minutes; turn dish one-quarter turn. Microwave until top springs back when touched lightly, 2 to 3 minutes. Immediately invert dish on serving plate. Let dish remain a minute so sauce drizzles over cake. Spread any remaining sauce over cake.

HOT FUDGE SUNDAE CAKE

1 cup all-purpose flour
¾ cup granulated sugar
2 tablespoons cocoa
2 teaspoons baking powder
¼ teaspoon salt
½ cup milk
2 tablespoons vegetable oil
1 teaspoon vanilla
1 cup chopped nuts (optional)
1 cup packed brown sugar
¼ cup cocoa
1¾ cups hot water

Mix flour, granulated sugar, 2 tablespoons cocoa, the baking powder and salt in 3-quart casserole. Stir in milk, oil and vanilla until smooth. Stir in nuts; sprinkle with brown sugar and ¼ cup cocoa.

Microwave water uncovered in 2-cup glass measure on high (100%) to boiling; pour over batter. Microwave uncovered on high (100%)

until cake is set but still glossy, 9 to 10 minutes, turning casserole one-quarter turn every 3 minutes. Serve with whipped cream or ice cream if desired.

9 servings.

Hot Fudge Butterscotch Sundae Cake: Substitute 1 package (6 ounces) butterscotch chips for the nuts. Decrease brown sugar to ½ cup and the ¼ cup cocoa to 2 tablespoons.

IMPOSSIBLE CHEESECAKE

1 cup milk
2 teaspoons vanilla
2 eggs
1 cup sugar
½ cup buttermilk baking mix
2 packages (8 ounces each) cream
    cheese, cut into about ½-inch cubes
    and softened
    Cheesecake Topping (below)

Grease 10-inch pie plate. Place milk, vanilla, eggs, sugar and baking mix in blender container. Cover and blend on high 15 seconds. Add cream cheese. Cover and blend on high 2 minutes. Pour into pie plate.

Microwave uncovered on inverted dinner plate on medium-high (70%) until filling is set, 12 to 18 minutes, turning pie plate one-quarter turn every 6 minutes. (Surface will be moist and sticky.) Cool on flat heatproof surface. Spread Cheesecake Topping carefully over top. Garnish with fruit if desired.

CHEESECAKE TOPPING
Mix 1 cup dairy sour cream, 2 tablespoons sugar and 2 teaspoons vanilla.

BANANA-TOPPED CAKE

½ package (18.5-ounce size) yellow cake
    mix with pudding (about 2 cups)
½ cup water
2 tablespoons vegetable oil
1 egg
¾ cup packed brown sugar
1 cup flaked coconut
⅓ cup chopped nuts
2 tablespoons milk
⅓ cup margarine or butter
2 medium bananas, sliced

Grease bottom only of oblong baking dish,
12 x 7½ x 2 inches. Beat cake mix, water, oil and
egg in large mixer bowl on low speed until
moistened. Beat on medium speed 2 minutes.
Pour batter into baking dish; spread evenly.

Microwave uncovered on high (100%) 4 minutes; turn dish one-half turn. Microwave until
wooden pick inserted in center comes out clean,
2½ to 3½ minutes. (Parts of the cake will appear
very moist, but these parts will continue to cook
while standing.) Cool thoroughly.

Mix brown sugar, coconut, nuts and milk in
1-quart casserole or bowl; add margarine. Microwave uncovered on high (100%) 2 minutes;
stir. Microwave until mixture boils and becomes
translucent, 1½ to 2 minutes.

Arrange bananas on cake. Spoon coconut topping over bananas, spreading to cover; cool.

PEANUT BUTTER ROCKY ROAD

1 package (6 ounces) semisweet
    chocolate chips
1 package (6 ounces) butterscotch chips
½ cup peanut butter
3 cups miniature marshmallows
½ cup salted peanuts

Place chocolate chips, butterscotch chips and
peanut butter in 2-quart bowl. Microwave uncovered on high (100%) until softened, 2 to 2½
minutes. Stir until melted and smooth.

Mix in marshmallows and peanuts until evenly
coated. Spread in buttered square baking pan,
8 x 8 x 2 inches. Refrigerate until firm, at least 1
hour. Cut into bars, 2 x 1 inch.

32 bars.

FRUIT-CEREAL CLUSTERS

1 pound white candy coating
1 cup chopped dried apricots
1 cup chopped dates
2 cups salted peanuts
2 cups corn puff cereal

Break candy coating into pieces in 4-quart casserole or bowl. Microwave uncovered on high
(100%) until softened, 4 minutes; stir. Microwave 1 minute. Stir until smooth. Stir in remaining ingredients until evenly coated. Drop by
tablespoonfuls onto waxed paper. Refrigerate
until set, 30 minutes to 1 hour.

About 4½ dozen clusters.

MINT-GLAZED BROWNIES

2 squares (1 ounce each) unsweetened
  chocolate
⅓ cup shortening
1 cup sugar
3 eggs
½ teaspoon vanilla
⅔ cup all-purpose flour
½ teaspoon baking powder
½ teaspoon salt
9 chocolate-covered mint patties

Grease round baking dish, 8 x 1½ inches. Microwave chocolate uncovered in 2-quart bowl on high (100%) until melted, 2 to 3½ minutes. Add shortening. Microwave until melted, 1 to 2 minutes. Beat in sugar, eggs and vanilla until smooth. Stir in flour, baking powder and salt. Spread evenly in baking dish.

Microwave uncovered on high (100%) 2 minutes; turn dish one-quarter turn. Microwave until set but not dry, 1½ to 2½ minutes. (Parts of dough will appear very moist, but these parts will continue to cook while standing.)

Place mint patties on brownies in 3 rows. Microwave uncovered until filling melts out around chocolate coating, 2 to 3½ minutes; spread over brownies. Cool; cut into bars, about 2 x 1½ inches.

20 brownies.

ROCKY ROAD BROWNIES

2 squares (1 ounce each) unsweetened
  chocolate
⅓ cup margarine or butter
1 cup sugar
2 eggs
½ teaspoon vanilla
½ cup all-purpose flour
½ teaspoon salt
¼ teaspoon baking powder
  Rocky Road Frosting (below)

Grease bottom only of square baking dish, 8 x 8 x 2 inches. Microwave chocolate and margarine uncovered in 2½-quart casserole or bowl on high (100%) until chocolate is softened, 1½ to 2 minutes. Stir until smooth. Mix in sugar, eggs and vanilla. Stir in flour, salt and baking powder. Spread evenly in baking dish.

Microwave uncovered 3 minutes; turn dish one-quarter turn. Microwave until no longer doughy, 2 to 3 minutes. Cool; frost with Rocky Road Frosting. Refrigerate to set frosting, about 30 minutes. Cut into about 1½-inch squares.

25 cookies.

ROCKY ROAD FROSTING
3 tablespoons margarine or butter
1 package (6 ounces) semisweet
  chocolate chips
1 tablespoon milk
1½ cups miniature marshmallows
⅓ cup chopped nuts

Microwave margarine and chocolate chips uncovered in bowl on high (100%) until chips are softened, 1 to 1½ minutes. Stir until smooth. Blend in milk. Stir in marshmallows and nuts until evenly coated.

PECAN BARS

¾ cup shortening (half margarine or
    butter, softened)
¾ cup powdered sugar
1½ cups all-purpose flour
½ teaspoon salt
2 eggs
1 cup packed brown sugar
2 tablespoons flour
½ teaspoon baking powder
½ teaspoon salt
½ teaspoon vanilla
1 cup chopped pecans

Mix shortening and powdered sugar thoroughly. Stir in 1½ cups flour and ½ teaspoon salt. Press mixture firmly in oblong baking dish, 11 x 7½ x 1½ inches.

Microwave uncovered on high (100%) 2 minutes; turn dish one-quarter turn. Microwave until no longer doughy, 2 to 3 minutes. Mix remaining ingredients; spread over hot layer. Microwave 3 minutes; turn dish one-quarter turn. Microwave 3 minutes. Cool; cut into bars, about 3 x 1 inch.

28 bars.

Chocolate-covered Pecan Bars: Immediately sprinkle warm bars with 1 package (6 ounces) semisweet chocolate chips. Microwave uncovered on high (100%) until chocolate is melted, about 1 minute; spread over bars.

PEANUT BUTTER BARS

¾ cup packed brown sugar
½ cup margarine or butter, softened
⅓ cup crunchy peanut butter
1 egg
1 teaspoon vanilla
1 cup all-purpose flour
¾ cup rolled oats
¼ teaspoon salt
    Peanut Butter Frosting (below)

Grease bottom only of oblong baking dish, 12 x 7½ x 2 inches. Mix brown sugar, margarine, peanut butter, egg and vanilla; stir in flour, oats and salt. Spread evenly in baking dish.

Microwave uncovered on high (100%) 3 minutes; turn dish one-half turn. Microwave until no longer doughy, 2 to 3 minutes. Cool; frost with Peanut Butter Frosting. If desired, refrigerate to set frosting. Cut into bars, about 2 x 1½ inches.

30 cookies.

PEANUT BUTTER FROSTING
⅓ cup crunchy peanut butter
1 package (6 ounces) butterscotch chips

Microwave peanut butter and butterscotch chips uncovered in 2-cup glass measure on high (100%) until softened, 1 to 1½ minutes. Stir until blended.

Pictured at left: Serve some prize winners. Clockwise from top — Pecan Bars (above), Frosted Lemon Treats (page 84) and Rocky Road Brownies (page 81).

FROSTED LEMON TREATS

½ cup margarine or butter, softened
¼ cup sugar
1 egg
1 teaspoon grated lemon peel
3 tablespoons milk
1¼ cups all-purpose flour
½ teaspoon baking powder
½ teaspoon salt
　Lemon Frosting (below)

Grease bottom only of oblong baking dish, 10 x 6 x 1½ inches. Mix margarine, sugar, egg, lemon peel and milk. Stir in flour, baking powder and salt. Spread evenly in baking dish.

Microwave uncovered on high (100%) 2 minutes; turn dish one-half turn. Microwave until no longer doughy, 1 to 2 minutes. Cool; frost with Lemon Frosting. Draw tines of fork through frosting. Cut into bars, about 2 x 1½ inches.

18 cookies.

LEMON FROSTING

3 tablespoons margarine or butter, softened
¾ cup powdered sugar
1 teaspoon lemon juice

Beat all ingredients until smooth.

CHOCOLATE CHIP SQUARES

½ cup packed brown sugar
½ cup margarine or butter, softened
1 egg
1 teaspoon vanilla
½ cup all-purpose flour
½ cup rolled oats
1 teaspoon baking powder
¼ teaspoon salt
⅓ cup semisweet chocolate chips
¼ cup chopped nuts

Grease bottom only of square baking dish, 8 x 8 x 2 inches. Mix brown sugar, margarine, egg and vanilla. Stir in flour, oats, baking powder

and salt. Spread evenly in baking dish. Sprinkle with chocolate chips and nuts.

Microwave uncovered on high (100%) 4 minutes; turn dish one-quarter turn. Microwave until no longer doughy, 2 to 3 minutes. Cool; cut into about 2-inch squares.

16 cookies.

CHEWY GRAHAM-COCONUT BARS

1 cup packed brown sugar
½ cup margarine or butter, softened
1 egg
¼ teaspoon vanilla
¾ cup all-purpose flour
¾ cup graham cracker crumbs (about 9 squares)
⅓ cup flaked coconut
¼ cup chopped nuts
¼ teaspoon salt

Grease bottom only of oblong baking dish, 12 x 7½ x 2 inches. Mix brown sugar, margarine, egg and vanilla. Stir in flour, graham cracker crumbs, coconut, nuts and salt. Spread evenly in baking dish.

Microwave uncovered on high (100%) 3 minutes; turn dish one-half turn. Microwave until wooden pick inserted in center comes out clean, 2 to 3 minutes. (Parts of dough will appear very moist, but these parts will continue to cook while standing.) Cool thoroughly; cut into bars, about 2 x 1½ inches.

30 cookies.

SOUPS, SANDWICHES AND SNACKS

POTATO SOUP

    4 slices bacon
    1 medium onion, chopped
    ½ cup water
    1 package (12 ounces) frozen shredded
         hash brown potatoes
 1 ½ teaspoons salt
    ⅛ teaspoon pepper
    3 tablespoons margarine or butter
         (optional)
    2 tablespoons flour
    2 cups milk
    1 cup water

Place bacon in 2½-quart casserole. Cover loosely and microwave on high (100%) until crisp, 4 to 5 minutes. Remove bacon from fat; drain bacon.

Add onion to bacon fat in casserole. Cover and microwave until onion is tender, 3 to 4 minutes.

Add ½ cup water and the frozen potatoes. Cover and microwave until potatoes are thawed, 6 to 7 minutes.

Stir in salt, pepper and margarine. Shake flour and milk in tightly covered jar; stir into potato mixture with 1 cup water. Cover and microwave 5 minutes; stir. Cover and microwave until mixture boils and thickens slightly, 3 to 5 minutes. Crumble bacon and sprinkle over top.

5 or 6 servings.

ZUCCHINI SOUP

    4 cups sliced zucchini (about 1 pound)
    1 small onion, chopped
    2 tablespoons margarine or butter
    1 can (10¾ ounces) condensed cream of
         chicken soup
    2 cups water
    1 teaspoon salt
    ½ teaspoon dried basil leaves
    ⅛ teaspoon pepper

Cover and microwave zucchini, onion and margarine in 2-quart casserole on high (100%), until vegetables are tender, 9 to 11 minutes.

Place soup, 1 cup of the water and the zucchini mixture in blender container. Cover and blend on medium-high speed until smooth, about 1 minute.

Return mixture to casserole. Stir in remaining 1 cup water, the salt, basil and pepper. Cover and microwave on high (100%) until hot and bubbly, 8 to 10 minutes. (Can be refrigerated and served cold.)

4 servings.

BEER-CHEESE SOUP

1 small onion, chopped
¼ cup margarine or butter
⅓ cup all-purpose flour
1 tablespoon instant chicken bouillon
3½ cups milk
1 jar (8 ounces) pasteurized process
   cheese spread
1 cup shredded Cheddar cheese (about
   4 ounces)
1 cup beer

Cover and microwave onion and margarine in 2-quart casserole on high (100%) until onion is tender, 3 to 4 minutes. Stir in flour and bouillon, then gradually stir in milk. Cover and microwave 6 minutes; stir. Cover and microwave to boiling, 3 to 5 minutes.

Stir in cheese spread, cheese and beer. Cover and microwave until hot and bubbly and cheese is melted, 3 to 4 minutes; stir.

5 or 6 servings.

ASPARAGUS-CHEESE CHOWDER

2 cups cubed potatoes (about
   2 medium)
½ cup sliced carrot
½ cup sliced celery
1 small onion, chopped
½ cup water
2 cups milk
¼ cup all-purpose flour
1½ teaspoons salt
¼ teaspoon pepper
¼ cup margarine or butter
1 can (15 ounces) cut asparagus
1 cup shredded Swiss cheese (about
   4 ounces)

Cover and microwave potatoes, carrot, celery, onion and water in 3-quart casserole on high (100%) until vegetables are tender, 10 to 12 minutes.

Shake milk, flour, salt and pepper in tightly covered jar; stir into vegetables. Add margarine.

Cover and microwave 3½ minutes; stir. Cover and microwave to boiling, 2 to 3 minutes.

Stir in asparagus (with liquid) and cheese. Cover and microwave until hot and bubbly and cheese is melted, 3 to 4 minutes. Stir.

5 or 6 servings.

HOT CHICKEN SALAD SANDWICHES

1½ cups cut-up cooked chicken
½ cup chopped celery
¼ cup chopped almonds or pecans
⅓ cup drained crushed pineapple
¼ cup mayonnaise or salad dressing
4 English muffins, split and toasted
   Avocado slices (optional)

Mix chicken, celery, almonds, pineapple and mayonnaise. Place muffins cut sides up on serving plate. Spread chicken mixture onto muffin halves, being careful to bring to edges.

Microwave uncovered on high (100%) until filling is warm, 1¼ to 2 minutes. Garnish with avocado slices.

4 servings.

Pictured at right: Make a snack or team up for a meal — Zucchini Soup (page 85), Hot Chicken Salad Sandwiches (above) and Caramel Corn (page 94)

BACON, CHEESE AND TOMATO SANDWICHES

3 slices bacon
3 slices rye bread, toasted
2 tablespoons mayonnaise or salad
   dressing
½ teaspoon dried dill weed
1 large tomato, sliced
3 slices Swiss cheese

Place bacon on microwave rack in glass dish. Cover loosely and microwave until crisp, 2½ to 3½ minutes.

Spread toast with mayonnaise; sprinkle with dill. Place toast slices on serving plate; top with tomato and cheese slices. Crumble bacon and sprinkle over top.

Microwave uncovered on high (100%) until cheese begins to melt, 1 to 1½ minutes.

3 sandwiches.

HAM AND CHEESE WITH COLESLAW

2 tablespoons margarine or butter
½ teaspoon prepared mustard
4 slices rye bread, toasted
4 slices cooked ham
1 large tomato, sliced
4 slices cheese
1 cup coleslaw

Microwave margarine uncovered in custard cup on high (100%) until softened, 15 to 30 seconds. Blend in mustard. Spread margarine on one side of each toast slice. Place slices buttered sides up on serving plate; top with ham, tomato and cheese slices.

Microwave uncovered until cheese begins to melt, 1½ to 2 minutes. Top each sandwich with a spoonful of coleslaw.

4 sandwiches.

SLOPPY FRANKS

1 small onion, chopped
⅓ cup chopped green pepper
1 tablespoon margarine or butter
½ cup barbecue sauce
¼ cup catsup
1 pound frankfurters, cut into
   ¼-inch slices
12 hamburger buns, split

Cover and microwave onion, green pepper and margarine in 1-quart casserole on high (100%) until vegetables are tender, 3 to 4 minutes.

Stir in barbecue sauce, catsup and frankfurters. Cover and microwave 2½ minutes; stir. Cover and microwave until mixture boils, 2 to 3 minutes.

Spoon mixture into buns on serving plate. Microwave uncovered on high (100%) until buns are hot, 1 to 2 minutes.

12 sandwiches.

CHILI DOGS

2 frankfurters
2 frankfurter buns, split
⅓ cup chili with beans

Microwave frankfurters uncovered on high (100%) until warm, 30 to 45 seconds. Place 1 frankfurter in each bun on serving plate; spoon chili onto frankfurters. Microwave uncovered until chili is hot, 1 to 1½ minutes.

2 sandwiches.

Note: If preparing just one chili dog, microwave uncovered 30 to 45 seconds.

HOBO BUNS

2 tablespoons mayonnaise or salad
     dressing
½ teaspoon prepared mustard
3 Kaiser or French rolls, split
3 slices bologna
1 large tomato, sliced
3 green pepper rings
3 slices cheese

Mix mayonnaise and mustard; spread over cut sides of rolls. Place bottom halves of rolls on serving plate. Top with bologna, tomato, green pepper, cheese and top halves of rolls.

Microwave uncovered on high (100%) until cheese begins to melt, 1 to 1½ minutes.

3 sandwiches.

BARBECUED BEEF ON BUNS

1 cup catsup
2 tablespoons brown sugar
1 tablespoon lemon juice
1 tablespoon Worcestershire sauce
1 teaspoon prepared mustard
½ teaspoon onion salt
⅛ teaspoon pepper
8 ounces thinly sliced cooked roast beef
     (8 to 10 slices)
4 hamburger buns, split

Mix catsup, brown sugar, lemon juice, Worcestershire sauce, mustard, onion salt and pepper in 2-cup glass measure. Microwave uncovered on high (100%) 1½ minutes; stir. Microwave to boiling, 1 to 2 minutes.

Layer half of the beef slices and half of the sauce in 1-quart casserole; repeat. Cover and microwave on high (100%) until hot and bubbly, 1½ to 2½ minutes.

Place bottom halves of buns on serving plate. Top with beef and remaining bun halves. Microwave uncovered on high (100%) until buns are hot, 30 seconds to 1 minute.

4 sandwiches.

BARBECUED BEEF IN CRUSTY ROLLS

⅓ cup catsup
2 tablespoons vinegar
2 tablespoons finely chopped onion
1 small clove garlic, finely chopped
1½ teaspoons Worcestershire sauce
1 teaspoon packed brown sugar
⅛ teaspoon dry mustard
     Dash of pepper
2 cups cut-up cooked beef
4 French rolls, split
4 slices process American cheese

Mix all ingredients except beef, rolls and cheese in 1-quart casserole. Cover and microwave on high (100%) until hot and bubbly, 2 to 3 minutes; stir. Mix beef into sauce. Cover and microwave until beef is hot, 3 to 5 minutes. Fill rolls with beef mixture and cheese slices.

4 sandwiches.

TUNA BUNS

2 hard-cooked eggs, chopped
1 can (6½ ounces) tuna, drained
1 package (4 ounces) shredded Cheddar
     cheese (about 1 cup)
¼ cup chopped green pepper
2 tablespoons finely chopped onion
½ teaspoon prepared mustard
½ cup mayonnaise or salad dressing
6 to 8 hamburger buns, split

Mix eggs, tuna, cheese, green pepper, onion, mustard and mayonnaise. Fill buns with tuna mixture. Place on serving plate.

Microwave uncovered on high (100%) until filling is warm, 1½ to 2 minutes.

6 to 8 sandwiches.

STORE-AND-SPOON BURGERS

1 pound hamburger
¼ cup chopped onion (optional)
¼ cup catsup
4 teaspoons prepared mustard
½ teaspoon salt
⅛ teaspoon pepper
½ cup shredded process cheese or
    Cheddar cheese (2 ounces)
8 hamburger buns, split

Crumble hamburger into 1-quart casserole; add onion. Microwave uncovered on high (100%) 4 minutes. Stir to break up meat. Microwave uncovered until meat is firm, 1 to 2 minutes; drain.

Stir in catsup, mustard, salt, pepper and cheese. Cover and refrigerate until ready to serve (can be stored up to 3 days).

To serve, spoon about ¼ cup meat mixture between bun halves. Microwave uncovered on serving plates until filling is hot:

    1 bun – 15 to 30 seconds
    2 buns – 30 to 45 seconds
    4 buns – 1 to 1½ minutes

8 sandwiches.

PIZZA BURGERS

1 pound hamburger
1 can (6 ounces) tomato paste
½ cup finely chopped pepperoni
1 slice bread, crumbled
1 teaspoon salt
½ teaspoon dried oregano leaves
    Dash of pepper
1 egg, beaten
    Sliced olives or onion or green pepper rings
1 cup shredded mozzarella cheese (about
    4 ounces)
8 hamburger buns, split

Mix hamburger, half of the tomato paste, the pepperoni, bread, salt, oregano, pepper and egg. Shape into 8 patties. Place in oblong baking dish, 12 x 7½ x 2 inches. Cover loosely and

microwave on high (100%) 6 minutes; turn dish one-half turn. Microwave until meat is firm, 4 to 5 minutes.

Spread cut sides of buns with remaining tomato paste. Place bottom halves of buns on serving plate. Place a patty on each bun half. Top with olives, cheese and top half of bun. Microwave uncovered on high (100%) until cheese begins to melt, 1½ to 2 minutes.

8 sandwiches.

QUICK CHEESE FONDUE

1 can (11 ounces) condensed Cheddar
    cheese soup
¼ cup dry white wine
    Dash of garlic powder
⅛ teaspoon Worcestershire sauce
½ cup shredded Swiss or Cheddar cheese
    (about 2 ounces)
    French bread, cut into 1-inch cubes

Mix soup, wine, garlic powder and Worcestershire sauce in 1-quart casserole. Cover and microwave on high (100%) 2½ minutes.

Stir in cheese. Microwave uncovered until mixture is smooth, 2½ to 3 minutes, stirring every minute. If desired, pour into fondue pot or chafing dish to keep warm. Use long-handled forks to spear bread cubes, then dip and swirl in fondue with a stirring motion.

4 or 5 servings.

CHILI FONDUE DIP

2 tablespoons margarine or butter
2 cups shredded sharp process American
   cheese (about 8 ounces)
3 to 5 drops red pepper sauce
⅓ cup dry white wine
1 can (4 ounces) whole green chilies,
   drained and chopped
   Dippers (green pepper, zucchini and
   celery sticks, cherry tomato halves,
   rye bread cubes)

Microwave margarine uncovered in 1½-quart bowl on high (100%) 30 seconds. Stir in cheese. Microwave 30 seconds; stir. Microwave 30 seconds longer.

Add pepper sauce; stir in wine slowly. Stir in chilies. Microwave until hot, 30 seconds. If desired, pour into fondue pot or chafing dish to keep warm. Use long-handled forks to spear Dippers, then dip and swirl in fondue with a stirring motion.

About 1½ cups dip.

Pepperoni Fondue Dip: Omit chilies. Stir in ¾ cup finely snipped pepperoni or salami and 1 small clove garlic, finely chopped, after stirring in the wine.

CLAM-PEPPER DIP

¼ cup chopped onion
¼ cup chopped green pepper
2 tablespoons margarine or butter
1 can (6½ ounces) minced clams, drained
1 cup shredded process American Cheese
   (about 4 ounces)
¼ cup catsup
2 teaspoons Worcestershire sauce

Cover and microwave onion, green pepper and margarine in 1-quart casserole on high (100%) until onion is tender, 3 to 4 minutes; stir.

Mix in remaining ingredients. Cover and microwave 1 minute; stir. Cover and microwave until cheese is melted, 1 to 2 minutes; stir.

About 2 cups dip.

STORE 'N HEAT CHEESE SPREAD

1 jar (2½ ounces) dried beef
1 cup water
1 package (8 ounces) cream cheese
¼ cup mayonnaise or salad dressing
¼ cup chopped green onions
2 teaspoons dried parsley flakes
2 cups shredded Cheddar cheese (about
   8 ounces)
   Assorted crackers
   Chopped nuts (optional)

Snip beef into small pieces. Combine beef and water in 2-cup glass measure. Microwave uncovered on high (100%) to boiling, 2 to 3 minutes; drain.

Microwave cream cheese uncovered in 1-quart bowl on high (100%) until softened, 30 to 45 seconds. Mix in beef, mayonnaise, green onions, parsley and cheese. Cover tightly and refrigerate up to 1 week.

To serve, spread a rounded tablespoonful of cheese mixture on each cracker; sprinkle with nuts. Place about 15 to 20 crackers on serving plate. Microwave uncovered on high (100%) until spread is warm, 30 seconds to 1 minute.

About 2½ cups spread.

Note: Spread can be divided in half and formed into 2 rolls, each about 12 inches long. Roll in nuts; wrap tightly and refrigerate. To serve, cut spread into ⅝-inch slices and place on crackers. Microwave as directed above.

BRIE WITH ALMONDS

- 1 whole round Brie cheese (4½ ounces)
- 2 tablespoons margarine or butter
- ¼ cup toasted sliced almonds
- 1 tablespoon brandy (optional)
  Assorted crackers

Microwave cheese uncovered on serving plate on medium (50%) just until soft and warm, 2 to 3 minutes.

Microwave margarine uncovered in dish on high (100%) until melted, about 1 minute. Stir in almonds and brandy; pour over cheese. Garnish with parsley if desired. Serve with crackers.

8 servings.

CHORIZO CHIPS

- 2 chorizo sausages (8 ounces)
  Tortilla chips
- ¾ cup shredded Cheddar cheese (about 3 ounces)

Crumble sausages into 1-quart casserole. Cover loosely and microwave on high (100%) until done, 2½ minutes; drain.

Place tortilla chips in single layer on 12-inch serving plate. Sprinkle sausages and cheese evenly over chips. Microwave uncovered on high (100%) until cheese is melted, 30 seconds to 1 minute.

4 servings.

A trio of savories for party-time and/or snack-time: Clockwise from left — Chorizo Chips (above), Chili Fondue Dip (page 91) and Brie with Almonds (above).

BEEF JERKY

1¼-pound beef boneless top round
¼ cup soy sauce
¼ cup water
1 tablespoon sugar
1 teaspoon garlic powder
1 teaspoon onion powder
¼ teaspoon red pepper sauce

Trim all fat and connective tissue from meat; discard. Freeze meat until partially frozen, about 1 hour. Cut steak diagonally across the grain into ⅛-inch slices. Mix remaining ingredients; stir in beef. Cover and refrigerate at least 1 hour; drain.

Arrange half of the meat close together on microwave roasting rack. Cover loosely and microwave on low (30%) 21 minutes. Arrange drier strips in center of rack; turn rack one-half turn. Microwave 21 minutes; turn rack one-half turn and microwave until dry but slightly pliable, about 10 minutes. Cool on waxed paper; cover with additional waxed paper. Repeat with remaining meat. Let stand 24 hours before storing.

About 48 slices.

FILLED TORTILLA SNACKS

⅔ cup chili with beans
2 flour tortillas
¼ cup shredded mozzarella cheese

Spoon chili down center of each tortilla; sprinkle with cheese. Fold sides of tortilla up over filling, overlapping edges. Microwave uncovered on serving plate on high (100%) until filling is hot, 1 to 1½ minutes.

2 snacks.

Note: If preparing just one tortilla, microwave 30 to 45 seconds.

BARBECUED BOLOGNA BITES

⅓ cup catsup
3 tablespoons molasses
2 tablespoons prepared mustard
1 tablespoon vinegar
2 teaspoons Worcestershire sauce
4 drops red pepper sauce
1 package (16 ounces) ring bologna, cut into ½-inch pieces

Mix catsup, molasses, mustard, vinegar, Worcestershire sauce and pepper sauce in 2-quart casserole; stir in bologna. Cover and microwave until bologna is hot, 2 to 3 minutes.

6 to 8 servings.

CORN CEREAL BALLS

4 cups crispy corn puff cereal
½ cup sugar
¼ cup dark corn syrup
1½ teaspoons margarine or butter
¼ teaspoon salt
1 teaspoon vanilla
Food color (optional)

Pour cereal into buttered 4-quart bowl. Mix sugar, corn syrup, margarine and salt in 4-cup glass measure. Microwave uncovered on high (100%) to rolling boil, 2 to 3 minutes.

Stir in vanilla and food color; pour over cereal in bowl, stirring until well coated. Shape firmly into 2-inch balls with buttered hands. Place about 2 inches apart on waxed paper. (Balls may need reshaping as they cool and become firm.)

About 1 dozen cereal balls.

GRAHAM-FRUIT PUFFS

Top graham cracker squares with banana or apple slices. Place squares on serving plate. Top each square with a large marshmallow. Microwave uncovered on high (100%) until marshmallow is puffed:

1 or 2 puffs — 15 to 30 seconds
3 or 4 puffs — 30 to 45 seconds

Top each puff with another cracker square.

Note: For extra heartiness, spread crackers with peanut butter before topping with fruit slices.

MALLOW-NUT CEREAL CLUSTERS

½ pound white candy coating
3 cups honey graham cereal
½ cup salted peanuts
½ cup miniature marshmallows

Break candy coating into small pieces in 2-quart casserole. Microwave uncovered on medium (50%) until softened, 3 to 4 minutes; stir until smooth and creamy.

Fold in cereal until completely coated. Stir in peanuts and marshmallows. Drop by rounded tablespoonfuls onto waxed paper or aluminum foil; shape into mounds with spoon. Let cool until firm, about 1 hour. Store in tightly covered container.

About 2 dozen clusters.

CARAMEL CORN

16 cups popped corn
1 cup packed brown sugar
½ cup margarine or butter
¼ cup light corn syrup
½ teaspoon salt
½ teaspoon baking soda

Divide popped corn between two 4-quart bowls.

Mix brown sugar, margarine, corn syrup and salt in 2½-quart casserole. Microwave uncovered on high (100%) 2½ minutes; stir. Microwave uncovered to boiling, 30 seconds. Boil 3 minutes.

Stir in baking soda. Pour syrup mixture on popped corn, stirring until mixed. Microwave uncovered on high (100%), one bowl at a time, until well coated, 2½ to 3½ minutes, stirring every minute. Cool, stirring occasionally.

16 cups caramel corn.

COOKED CARAMEL-APPLE SLICES

2 caramels
1 medium apple, sliced

Place a caramel in each of 2 custard cups. Divide apple slices between dishes. Microwave uncovered on high (100%) until apple is tender, 2 to 3 minutes. Stir to coat apple slices with caramel. Serve warm.

2 snacks.

INDEX